Elementary School Libraries

Second Edition

by

Jean Elizabeth Lowrie, Ph.D.

The Scarecrow Press, Inc.
Metuchen, N.J.　　　1970

Copyright 1970, by Jean Elizabeth Lowrie
SBN 8108-0305-4

Acknowledgements

Grateful acknowledgement is made to Miss Harriet G. Long, Professor, to Miss Hannah Hunt, Assistant Professor, to Miss Elizabeth Gross, Assistant Professor, and to Dr. Jesse Shera, Dean, the School of Library Science, to Mrs. Ilse Forest, Visiting Lecturer in Education, the School of Education and to Dr. John Dickhoff, Dean, Cleveland College, Western Reserve University, for their advice and assistance.

Sincere appreciation is expressed to the following librarians and supervisors for arranging the visits within their respective school systems: Mrs. Alice Brooks McGuire, Librarian, Casis School, Austin, Texas; Mrs. Fay Holly, Curriculum Coordinator, Jackson, Tennessee; Miss Virginia McJenkins, Director, Fulton County School Libraries, Atlanta, Georgia; Miss Sara Jaffarian, Director of Libraries, Greensboro, North Carolina; Miss Elizabeth D. Hodges, Supervisor of Library Services, Baltimore County Board of Education, Towson, Maryland; Miss Christine Gilbert, Coordinator of School-Community Relations, Manhasset, New York; Miss Genevieve Fancher, Assistant Consultant of Elementary School Libraries, Jamestown, New York; Miss Mildred Winslow, Librarian, Cossitt School, La Grange, Illinois; Mrs. Harriette H. Crummer, Supervisor of Children's Library Service, Evanston, Illinois; Miss Hazel Brown, Librarian, Longfellow School, Royal Oak, Michigan; to the following people who aided in the selection of the school systems visited: Miss Mildred Batchelder, Executive Secretary of the Children's Library Services Division, American Library Association; Miss Louise Galloway, Assistant Professor, Library School, State University, Tallahassee, Florida; Miss Mary V. Gaver, Professor, Graduate School of Library Service, Rutgers University, New

Brunswick, New Jersey; Mrs. Jane B. Hobson, formerly School Library Consultant, Public and School Library Services Bureau, Department of Education, Trenton, New Jersey; Miss Anna Clark Kennedy, New York State Department of Education; Mrs. Mariana McAllister, formerly Interim Executive Secretary, the American Association of School Librarians, American Library Association; Miss Crystal McNally, Coordinator Elementary School Libraries, Wichita, Kansas; Miss Louise Meredith, Supervisor of School Libraries, State Department of Education, Nashville, Tennessee; Miss Mildred L. Nickel, formerly Director of School Libraries, State Department of Public Instruction, Springfield, Illinois; Miss Elinor Yungmeyer, School Library Consultant, Michigan State Library, Lansing, Michigan. Appreciation is expressed also to the faculties, administrators and consultants for the cooperation and hospitality extended during the visitations in their respective schools. Deep appreciation is expressed also to my Mother and Father who encouraged beyond measure the fulfillment of this study.

In this study quotations which are of a general nature or ones which are repeated by several people are not documented. Documentation is given, however, for those comments which represent personal viewpoints or seem to be of particular significance or uniqueness.

The visits and observations in this study were made possible in part by the Dutton Macrae award presented to the writer by the American Library Association in 1957. This material support, which manifests the interest in the development of children's library services by a publishing house, is a significant contribution in the field of library research and study.

Jean Elizabeth Lowrie
1960.

Preface, 1969

It is exactly ten years since the initial study culminating in a book on elementary school libraries was completed, and the growth in service and in number of elementary school libraries since then has been phenomenal. With the increasing emphasis on total media center programs, it is quite evident that the impact of legislation, new materials of communication, functional library instruction, etc., require changes and additions in this presentation. A deliberative effort has been made in this new edition to include a broad spectrum of schools--representative of large metropolitan programs, of county and city systems, of small rural schools, of demonstration centers, of "regular" school libraries, of communities with high tax support and upper-middle socio-economic level, of communities where the majority of the inhabitants are poor (both black and white). It is increasingly important to stress that elementary library service is for the disadvantaged at every level--cultural, economic, intellectual.

There were three definite areas in which obvious changes had taken place and which, therefore, needed to be examined in some depth: (1) new approaches in library instruction; (2) new attitudes toward flexible scheduling in library uses; and (3) broader understanding of the phrase "total media center." In addition, greater emphasis is given to service at the primary level and in some instances at the pre-school level.

The emphasis on curriculum support and reading experience continues to be the basis of this study and indeed of school library service. The expansion of the collections, the flexibility of programming and the use of technological support provide the new approach and broaden the foundation for the basic "raison d'être."

A sabbatical in the winter of 1968, plus earlier visits to various parts of the country, provided the opportunity to revisit some of the original schools and to see new programs in others. The following systems have provided up to date material: Fulton County Schools, Fulton County, Georgia; Greensboro Public Schools, Greensboro, North Carolina; Montgomery County Schools, Montgomery County, Maryland; Bowman School, Lexington, Massachusetts; School #219, Queens, New York City Public Schools; Casis School, Austin, Texas; Wichita Public Schools, Wichita, Kansas; Houston Public Schools, Houston, Texas; Phoenix Public Schools, Districts #7, 8, 9, 10; District #110, Prairie Village, Kansas; Campus Elementary School, Western Michigan University, Kalamazoo, Michigan.

Appreciation is expressed to all the librarians, library supervisors, teachers and administrators who have welcomed me into their schools and who have so generously shared program materials and time. It is these people and all the other dedicated librarians who are basically responsible for the phenomenal growth in elementary school library service today.

Table of Contents

Acknowledgements ... iii

Preface, 1969 ... v

Chapter

I. Introducing the Elementary School Library ... 11
    Philosophy
    Scope and Services

II. Curriculum Supportive Experiences in the Middle Grades ... 20
    Overall Pattern of Library Practices
        Function of the library
        Classroom and library planning
        Using the library materials
        Variety in library resources
    Specific Curriculum Practices
        Social studies
        Science
        Other curriculum areas
    Services to Special Groups
        Gifted children
        Slow learners
        Physically handicapped children
        Disadvantaged

III. Reading Guidance in the Middle Grades ... 60
    Library Program
        Individual guidance
        Group guidance
    Classroom Programs
        Fourth grades
        Fifth grades
        Sixth grades

        Poetry Appreciation
        Creative Expression
        Reading records
        Book reports

IV. "How Do I Find ---?"   99
        Library Instruction
        Reference Work

V. Early Elementary Library Experiences 122

VI. The Teacher and the School Library 144
        Significant Areas for Teacher-Librarian
            Cooperation
        Teachers' Background in Children's
            Literature

VII. Role of the School Administrator 153
        Administrative Philosophy
        Administrative Responsibility
        Administrative Ideas for Expansion of
            Library Program

VIII. Auxiliary Features 169
        Publicity
        Schedules
        Student Assistants
        Media Services
        Physical Quarters

IX. Community Relationships 191
        Parent Relationships
            Assistance from parents
            Assistance to parents
        Public Library Cooperation
        Other Community Agencies

X. Elementary School Libraries are Realities 210
        Summary of Library Services
        Recommendations for Further
            Implementation
        Conclusion

Children's Books Mentioned in Text   218

Bibliography   223

Index   231

List of Tables

Table

1. Placement Chart for Teaching the Appreciation of Good Books and the Use of the Library 102

2. The "200's" 110

3. The Dewey Decimal Wheel 111

Chapter I

Introducing the Elementary School Library

> With its background of over fifty years of public library children's work and an equal inheritance of secondary school libraries and growing out of the needs of modern curriculums, the elementary school library is in a unique position today.[1]

Ten years later this statement is still true. The impact of federal legislation, the widespread use of all communication media at home and in school, the proliferation of knowledge, and the publication of the 1960 and 1969 Standards have all directed attention anew to the unique contributions which may be made by an elementary school library-media center in today's educational program.

Education today is confronted by many demands, criticisms both negative and positive, suggestions for drastic reorganization of programs. Although it is not the purpose of the writer to weigh these demands or attempt solutions of the programs, it is pertinent to point out the relationship between certain areas of concern and the role of the elementary school library. There is today a renewed emphasis on the need to arouse intellectual curiosity, to encourage research, to help the exceptional or gifted, to understand and assist the socio-economically deprived youngster, to stimulate understanding and use of the basic skills. In all these areas, the elementary school librarians believe they make definite contributions. For example, a library, with a full-time professional librarian, can assist a first-grade child in his beginning "research" efforts—"What's this bug I've caught?"; can capitalize on and spur a fifth- or sixth-grade boy's intense interest in aerodynamics or nuclear physics; can stimulate international and interracial understanding by presenting the right stories with the correct information to a group of middle-grade children who have become conscious of differences and need guidance toward creating empathy and impartial judgment; can provide a book which aids in developing reading skills for practical needs. Such services would appear to be of specific help in the process of developing mentally alert, emotionally balanced future citizens in a democratic nation.

 The growth of the elementary school library program over the past three decades has been tremendous. It has become a segment of the modern elementary school program which has more than justified its existence in situations where it has been allowed to come to fruition. This can be attributed to research in child growth and development, to new methods of teaching, and to changes in the concepts of school library service.

 Statistics in the latest biennial survey[2] indicate that 44.4 percent of elementary schools have centralized libraries; of these, 50.8 percent are served by school librarians and 50.1 percent include audio visual materials in their collection. This is a real growth over the 1957 report which indicated only a little more than 25 percent (28.89) of the elementary schools in the country were served by libraries. The trend is gratifying, but there are still many educators, Boards of Education and, unfortunately, some school librarians who are not fully aware of the functions and services of the elementary school library. There is still a need to provide a picture of some of the programs in existence, to ascertain if the overall philosophy is sufficiently flexible and virile, and to suggest some future developments.

 The phrase "every child needs a school library" has now attained nationwide significance. But to understand the raison d'être behind this ideal, it is necessary to have an understanding of the importance and the uniqueness of this type of library service. This may be acquired by reading recent articles in

Introduction

professional journals, both library and educational, and the perusal of curriculum guide books, library manuals and similar materials which present some firm aims and standards toward which the elementary school librarian should be striving. Such material also mentions specific functions and services which exemplify the unique position of the elementary school library and emphasizes the coexistent responsibilities of the teachers and administrators in this total library program. All of these reveal crystallization of the concept that a library is total in service and total in materials.

It has been said that the "first objective of education everywhere is to induct the young into membership of their group, community or nation by transmitting to them their social heritage or that part of the culture pattern that will enable them to live in association with their fellow-citizens, and to have a feeling of belongingness."[3] Schools in the United States, accordingly, attempt to provide opportunities for each child to grow in social usefulness and to develop his intellectual interests and capabilities in order to insure his becoming a responsible member of society and, in each situation where there is a school library, its services have become an integral part of the program. "No phase of the entire school program is in a more strategic position to foster self learning and to bring meaning and understanding of the ever widening community than the school library."[4]

The philosophy which underlies the elementary school library in today's schools is based on a combination of good practices in library service to children and an acknowledgement of the needs of the curriculum in our modern program of elementary education. "The school library is a means to an end, not an end in itself. Its aims and philosophy are those of the school it serves."[5]

If the "aim of education is the realization of one's best self and greatest social efficiency and wide reading, consultation of varied references, [and if] investigation of many sources of information is necessary,"[6] the elementary school library is indispensable. If it is the "responsibility of the school to instill in children a life long love of books, to steep them in their heritage of great books, to enable them to use books and libraries for information and enlightenment,"[7] the elementary school library is indispensable. If it is also the responsibility of education to challenge the attitudes, the capabilities, the self understanding of youth, then it is the school librarian's responsibility to make use of all methods of communication to achieve this goal. Furthermore, "it is through school library experience of a community service nature as well as through the library's information and recreation resources that some students find self-realization, gain insight in human relations, have practical illustrations of economic efficiency and take action as responsible citizens."[8]

It is the function of the elementary school library, then, to assist the child to interpret himself in relation to others and develop in him a better understanding of life about him, to arouse true intellectual curiosity, to introduce to him his rich cultural heritage and to instill understanding of the intrinsic importance of reading and libraries in an informed nation.

The scope of the elementary school library program is broad and deep. The library is unique in that it gives service to all school personnel from the kindergarten child to administrator, from the mentally retarded to the gifted. The school library as it is conceived today is "that place in the school where a full range of materials and accompanying services are accessible to teachers and students. It represents a unified program involving both audio-visual and printed resources with a single administrative organization and with a staff of competent specialists."[9] The instructional materials included in such a center are "all types ...used in intellectual pursuits by teachers and students."[10] It should serve therefore as a coordinating agency aiding improved pupil achievement, improved teaching and creating richer experiences for both.

     The librarian works toward the achievement of this program in two major interlocking areas: (1) curriculum enrichment, and (2) reading for pleasure. She serves specifically as a coordinating factor in curriculum experimentation. The librarian is responsible for seeing that instruction is given to students in order that they may readily locate needed materials. She must be in close touch with the teacher so that the reference work, whether done in the classroom or in the library, will be meaningful. She must be aware of the subjects for study, the approach of the teacher, the interests of the children. The "school librarian sees the curriculum as a whole and is in a position to observe its strengths and weaknesses, its omissions and duplication," says one administrator. "Her special knowledge of materials of all kinds, their sources and availability, their appropriateness in terms of subject, treatment, and readability, equips her to make an essential and unique contribution to the development of the school program. To vitalize and implement each unit she is ready to suggest new editions of books to replace old ones, new titles to replace those outdated, easy materials for the slow learner, advanced materials for the gifted student and newer types of instructional media including audiovisual and community resources. This is an important service which must be rendered if the curriculum is to be active and dynamic, and if it is to provide for individual differences, thereby becoming meaningful to every pupil."[11]

     "Wherever school systems undertake a cooperative study and evaluation of the reading program in each grade, the library is the one unifying factor which can dramatically demonstrate its contribution at every level. No teacher in the school has a greater obligation than the school librarian to the reading program, nor a greater opportunity to see that reading becomes a delightful experience, meaningful, enriching and satisfying to every child."[12] The librarian is alert to encourage and provide for the wide reading interests which children pursue and attempts to find materials on their reading levels. She also makes it possible for the teacher to experiment in the teaching of reading, as in the individualized program, by providing a wide variety of materials for the classroom and by aiding in guidance of the individual pupil in the library. In both the area of curriculum enrichment and reading for pleasure, the library program in the elementary school also attempts to develop attitudes of good citizenship, such as an understanding of the care and sharing of public property, the assumption of personal responsibility and the importance of an orderly arrangement of materials.

The value of the centralized library over the limited classroom collection is stressed by both teachers and administrators. One teacher has expressed herself most succinctly on this point. It is "not possible--or desirable--for each classroom to house all instructional materials needed, even for one unit. Expense and necessity for sharing materials with other classrooms would make this practice prohibitive..... When children participate in the planning, evaluating, and replanning of activities, the teacher cannot predict the exact turn a unit will take. The library must be tapped for additional materials. Moreover, the library's orderly arrangement of extensive material makes it an essential adjunct to the classroom. . .where children can develop the ability to locate materials and use them independently. It is an important provision for the needs and interests of exceptional children in the class--particularly the gifted learners."[13]

"Room libraries would not be a happy situation," states another teacher. "I need the variety from a centralized collection and the use of many reference books. The library is basic to the teaching program."[14] An administrator lends support to this by stating that no classroom collection can provide adequate variety of materials. The only possible answer is a pooling

Introduction

of the school's resources in order that they can be available where and when they are needed. A central collection from which materials are constantly flowing to and from the classroom--materials having a particular purpose--this is the service a school library can give.[15]

Nor is it possible for the children's rooms in public libraries or for bookmobiles, both of which have important functions, to provide the variety of materials and immediate service that teachers and pupils in today's schools find necessary. Other types of library services may supplement or complement; they may promote the establishment of the elementary school library, but the essential ingredient of an adequate library program is the center within the school.

The scope, the service, the uniqueness of this program, however, rest primarily on the cooperative efforts of teachers and administrators with the librarian. The understanding shown through adequate financial support, through cooperative planning in the use of materials, through stimulating students to become effective library users; the constant use of the library as a center for reading pleasure, a source for individual informational needs; the acceptance of the librarian as a regular member of the faculty and an important contributor to curriculum planning--all of this is necessary for the development of the enriched library program for elementary school children.

This school library philosophy is widely accepted, but there is a need to know more about implementation of the elementary school library programs. The presentation of situations which have been judged representative of good elementary school library practices would appear to be of value. These may well serve as goals for those librarians just beginning to establish such a program; as suggestions for librarians and teachers now laboring in the field who are constantly seeking new ideas; as incentives for teachers and administrators who are considering organizing such a program; as stimulation for prospective teachers and librarians who are interested in knowing the contributions and possibilities of this service; and, perhaps, as an introduction for those outside the educational profession who are curious as to why this service should be considered of unique importance to the total elementary school program.

References

1. Sattley, Helen R. "The Credo of School Librarians." Saturday Review, 40:74, Nov. 16, 1957.

2. Darling, Richard L. Public School Library Statistics, 1962-63. Dept. of Health, Education and Welfare, U.S. Office of Education, 1964. p. 4.

3. Kandel, I. L. The New Era in Education: A Comparative Study. Boston, Houghton Mifflin, 1955. p. 48.

4. Falk, Philip H. "Changes in School Library Service to Meet Changes in School Programs." ALA Bulletin, LI:266, April, 1957.

5. "School Library Bill of Rights." School Libraries, VI:22-3, March, 1957.

6. "Library Manual." Evanston School District No. 65, Evanston, Illinois. n.p. (mimeographed.)

7. Arbutus School, Baltimore, Maryland.

8. American Library Association. Committee on Postwar Planning. School Libraries for Today and Tomorrow. Chicago, American Library Association, 1945. p. 6.

Introduction 19

9. American Association of School Librarians.
   <u>Standards for School Media Programs.</u>
   Chicago, American Library Association,
   1969, p. xv.

10. "News from the Knapp School Library Project."
    American Library Association, 1966.
    (Statement by Project's Advisory Committee.)

11. Willis, Benjamin C. "School Librarian: Coordinator." <u>ALA Bulletin,</u> LI:92, Feb., 1955.

12. <u>Ibid.</u>, p. 92.

13. Wortham, Josephine "The Library - A Classroom Must." <u>ALA Bulletin,</u> XLIX:59, Feb., 1955.

14. Plandome Road School, Manhasset, New York.

15. Dorsey, Grace A. "School Libraries in Maryland." <u>Maryland School Bulletin,</u> XXXIII: No. 2:7-9, June, 1954. Baltimore, Maryland State Dept. of Education.

Chapter II

Curriculum Supportive Experiences

in the Middle Grades

In this age of scientific interest, of awareness of one's neighbors at home and abroad and of increased leisure time, a tremendous amount of material is necessary to serve the needs of the child, whose development is being affected by the same influences which are molding adult thought and action. Furthermore, the impact of the mass media has opened broad interests to the younger children. Discussion of such subjects as interplanetary space, United Nations meetings, Afro-Asian tensions, aluminum mining, nuclear physics and early Western pioneers are common in elementary classrooms.

Among the commonly accepted goals of today's elementary schools are some that apply to the library program as well: (1) broadening concept of the classroom to include all types of living experiences, from the family to the international community; (2) the evaluative use of many sources of information; (3) small groups and individual, as well as class, learning activites; (4) acceptance of children as they are and provision of materials which take into consideration their individual differences; (5) emphasis on a problem-solving approach rather than on a memorization of facts; (6) acknowledgement of "persistent life situations" of which all children are aware and about which their curiosity increases as they mature; (7) an awareness of the need to develop among children the understanding that education is a lifelong process. All of these factors enter into the cooperative planning of teacher and librarian when studying the curriculum needs of the children.

Curriculum Support

One of the chief purposes of the elementary school library is to assist in a balanced reading program (basal, recreation, corrective curriculum). The enrichment of the teaching environment through reading for information has always been implemented by the school library. In today's technological world, however, there are many other media of communication, and the location, organization and dissemination of all media as they may relate to curriculum is an integral part of the school library. In this chapter on curriculum support, therefore, it is the intention to emphasize not only the reading or book contribution but the total media center contribution. The aspect of books for pleasure with breadth in reading interests has been allocated to a separate chapter.

It has been recognized that children must now develop an ability to read books, to use reference and factual materials, to listen and view, to evaluate and select in order to make adequate use of the materials which can convey information or develop skills and help guide evaluative thinking in any area of the curriculum. The elementary school librarian is faced with the responsibility of assisting teachers to guide their pupils in applying reading, viewing and listening skills in making use of the library's full resources.

Both teachers and students have commented favorably on the use of the library for the above purpose. Teachers have indicated their belief in the value of the centralized library in the elementary school and its relation to all phases of the school curriculum.

> Our library is a strong part of the school program and the librarian gives individual help whenever needed. I always go straight to the library for information when any question comes up.[1]

We could not teach social living without the library.[2]

Children's replies, when asked how they used their libraries for informational needs, have equal significance. A fifth-grade group, in responding to the question, "Why do you come to the library?" replied:

1. to get more knowledge;
2. to find answers to questions;
3. to look up something you don't understand;
4. to use the unabridged dictionary;
5. to come for books on our unit work.[3]

"How do you use the library?" a teacher asked her fourth-graders. "To make reports, to find books on Egypt, to look in the card catalog, to get flag and map pictures, for information on different countries, for information on different kinds of people, for stories, records and poems," came the varied replies.[4]

In one room in a discussion on "Ways we have learned how to study independently," the children explained how they had looked for information on the parts of a flower and on how seeds travel. "We used reference books that weren't too hard so we wouldn't goof up on understanding," said one boy, as he pointed out The Golden Treasury of Natural History, Seeds and Seed Travels, and Plants in the City. "We want to learn a lot so we get lots of books. We like to share what we learn with other rooms too."[5]

Such statements can be supported by specific examples of how the library enriches the curriculum, ways in which teachers and librarians work together to promote the use of the materials, and ways in which the children benefit from this service.

Curriculum Support   23

The statements on library practices and attitudes made by all the teachers and librarians visited present a rather uniform pattern: (1) the general function of the library; (2) the need for teacher, pupil, librarian planning before and after the library visit as well as in the library; (3) techniques for the presentation and use of the library materials; (4) special values from the variety of library resources. Some amplification of this pattern follows here, with further illustrations which describe specific practices in different subjects and grade levels, including services of the library to the gifted, slow, disadvantaged and handicapped children.

Overall Pattern of Library Practices

"The library," said one teacher, "is a supplementary collection for all unit work. We try to teach the use of many sources and how to understand different opinions. It is not just the availability of subject matter which is important. The library materials also give us an opportunity to teach other values too, such as accuracy, honesty, and forming one's own opinion. It is good to let the child explore for himself among the books and to learn to choose what may be helpful to him."[6]

The library has significant functions in relation to each grade's learning progress. In the fourth grade the children are becoming interested in finding out more about many things. The teacher must be constantly looking for resources that will help them. She does this searching with the librarian to help her. Fifth-graders are beginning to look for the real story about a person, facts, and "a whole book" about things. The teacher must establish the idea that there is not "a book" about everything. She must continue to help broaden the primary concept of "a" and "I" and begin to lead to searching and to more reflective answers. By the time the boys and girls are in the sixth grade, teachers expect them to be well grounded in the use of library books and materials and in the processes of search. In all grades gifted students are dependent upon library materials to challenge their abilities and to broaden their interests. Slower students, too, should have the opportunity to visit the library and learn to find books which they can read. Both groups should have time and occasion to develop library habits and competencies.

The majority of teachers questioned prefer to have materials organized in a library center. But the answer to the question, "Where should reference work be done?" continues to be determined by the needs of the classroom at that particular moment. Reference materials per se seem to be used more in the library center since they are of temporary interest and need not necessarily be charged out. Materials which need careful examination and may serve as the basis of work for many days are apparently evaluated in the center first, and then are circulated to the teacher or student or committee who wishes to use them in the classroom. There seems little need for reserve shelves in the library, at least below the middle school level. Whatever method is used, the stress continues to be laid on the availability of the materials to the children whenever they need them.

Planning by the teacher with the librarian is basic to good library use. The teacher must indicate the special emphases in order to determine the library instruction needed in preparation for reference work and in some cases the special media which must be available. Forewarning the librarian of subject needs will prevent frustration on the part of everyone. It is equally good cooperation for the teacher to come to the library with the class whenever possible. "Preplanning with the librarian cannot be stressed too much!" commented all teachers.

As a general rule, neither teacher nor librarian should give exact resources or references. Child-

Curriculum Support

ren need to be encouraged to do part of the searching by themselves, a bit of "psychology of learning through frustration," as one teacher expressed it. This is particularly true with fifth- and sixth-graders. One text cannot answer all the questions in connection with which the children help organize a unit. In many cases, a text is used for a basic background, a list of supplemental material and pertinent questions is complied, and the teacher and children go to the library. The children should search first, and then the librarian and the teacher assist them. In some instances the librarian chooses materials for the classroom collection, but usually individual students prefer to select their own books for room use.

An equally significant part of the program for using the library facilities adequately is the pre-planning which is done in the classroom. It is important when introducing a new topic to "let us see how many books we can find" and "to talk about this before going to the library." In preparing to use the library for reports, one teacher listed "what we want to know." She then reviewed and reminded the class "how we look up things" in the card catalog, indexes, tables of contents. She encouraged the idea of leafing through the book carefully and using many sources of information, not just one encyclopedia.[7] A fourth-grade group jots down reminders from suggestions by the whole class, even though only a few individuals may be going to the library at that time. They note places to look for sources, and facts they would like to know. "Beyond that," said the teacher, "they're on their own. The additional information often forthcoming shows good initiative."[8] Assuredly such consistent preparation prior to the library visit is the key to this next point in library service.

Using the library materials. When reading or viewing for curriculum enrichment there should be a purpose. Guiding questions and a search for definite information is necessary, otherwise there is a tendency toward meaningless copying.

All teachers emphasize the importance of learning how to take notes from library materials. In the fourth grade, the children often copy because the encyclopedia is hard for them to comprehend. The teacher is responsible for subsequent explanation and discussion of the reports in the room. One teacher explained that this "process of reporting is like building a house. One uses basic plans or sentences and then builds a new structure." She amplified this idea by reading a paragraph to the class and asking them to write what they thought it told.[9] Another teacher encouraged the use of pictures to help explain the report, eliminating the need to copy extensively. Many fourth- and fifth-grade teachers frequently start with the basic book and pick out the highlights, and there is much group work along this line at the beginning of the year. It is important for the teachers to guard against generalizations and to encourage children to look for facts. The librarian should be aware of the techniques that the teacher is using so that she too may lead the child to interpretation in his own words of the material read.

It is of equal importance that boys and girls understand how to use other media for note taking. For example notes may be taken by transferring pictures, graphs or diagrams to transparencies for sharing with the class. Many classroom teachers expected "a visual" to be used by the student in reporting. It might be a filmstrip or a tape checked out of the media center, or a transparency made by the student. There is a real effort on the part of teachers and librarians to orient boys and girls to the total media concept in their specific learning experiences as well as in their leisure time activities and informal learning experiences.

The great danger lies in a forced or structured use, but as all groups become less afraid of the equipment and more aware of the benefits of amalgamation of all software, total use will become a natural part of the learning environment.

"It is helpful," said one fifth-grade teacher, "to give some organization around which to build the report. For example, what is the problem; how did it arise; how did it come out?" She encouraged the children to use books by checking the index, reading and scanning, making quick notes before turning to the next title. The compilation of the notes taken might be supplemented with pictures, filmstrips and other books. The children learned not to rely on one person's opinion.[10]

Another teacher who expected her children to use from three to six reference books, depending upon the reading level of the child, stressed variety in the books consulted. It is good "to guide reports by asking a nice group of questions both specific and abstract." Suggestions to help the children to break away from copying were: (1) read and read and read; (2) talk and discuss with the group; (3) keep from writing as long as possible; (4) ask the general question and then specific ones; (5) jot down the main thought; (6) make a summary statement and evaluation. This teacher emphasized that it is important to begin to develop scholarly attitudes early.[11]

Sixth-grade teachers stress these same techniques and emphasize how to integrate notes. Children need help from teacher and librarian in picking out similarities. In one room the teacher gave her students basic information on the life of Nehru and they, in turn, searched for additional information. In another the students were attempting to learn how to evaluate content. Each one chose a topic of interest to him. Thermofax copies of articles from encyclopedias and other reference books were made. The materials were both good and bad, i.e. from the point of view of writing. Students evaluated the content to see whether this was usable material; could it be used for note taking; what was the pattern of organization; were the facts relevant to the topic? The same practice was used with tapes and recordings to develop standards for listening, specifically in relation to the topic of interest. This experience was carefully planned in advance by the faculty. McCullar's <u>How To Study and Why</u> was the basis for preparation in guiding children and teaching this type of evaluation.[12] The importance of outlining, of checking sources and learning about bibliographic methods, of scanning and comparing is stressed by all intermediate teachers with the scope increased as the understanding of the group matures.

In many schools both social studies and science notebooks were in evidence. These combined what was learned from reading matter covered in classroom work and contained a table of contents, a simplified bibliography, information on basic topics plus special interests and, occasionally, notes on classmate's reports.

In one class each child had a special topic, not too broad, on which to do a thorough search. This class was divided into three groups--one worked on art, another on reference, the third in reading. The groups alternated regularly.[13] This is a technique used by teachers in many schools for it provides opportunity for extensive small group reference work in the library and teachers can work with the individuals in the groups. "When a child has taken time to really work, he deserves the consideration of the teacher and the respect of the class in relation to his report, no matter what the subject area is," said one teacher.[14] "Report sharing is enjoyed by children."

<u>Variety in library resources.</u> Variety in materials being examined is encouraged by both teachers and librarians. Searching beyond basic and supplementary texts is emphasized. Children and teachers,

Curriculum Support

for instance, check the "books to enjoy" lists which appear at the end of the chapters in the social studies textbooks. Children preview, order and share filmstrips and movies which supplement the unit materials including work in arithmetic. They learn to use maps and atlases and vertical file materials. Magazines become an important source for background material, and the librarian emphasizes the value of articles for purposeful reading.

"There are so many good books, it is a shame to just be dependent on the encyclopedia," said a fifth grade teacher.[15] In another school the teacher suggested that the children go to the library for "research" first because there was an encyclopedia in the room and many children had them in their homes.[16] A consistent refrain from Texas to Maryland to Illinois was this need to be sure that children are led to other books and that the encyclopedias do not become "the end all and be all." This is not to say that encyclopedias are unimportant. They bring together much general information under subjects for which children constantly ask. They gather specific details which are not answered or are difficult to locate in other books. The point to be stressed here is that children need to learn that there are many places to which to go to learn the answers and to find information. Most important, they must learn to draw their own conclusions from these sources so that, ultimately, as adults, they may achieve independence from any one book, magazine or commentator in forming their own conclusions.

One of the printed aids which teachers are finding of more and more value in unit studies is the fiction book. Often fiction can increase interest and information at the same time. It is useful for historical background and atmosphere. Frequently, these books are read aloud by the teachers. A sixth-grade teacher, for example, included Gift of the Golden Cup in her study on Roman life. The use of a story, however, requires guidance in helping the children to understand its use for background information. Children often feel that this is "hard to do" or "it takes too long to read a whole book." They should be assisted to look for the place where the scene is laid, the descriptions of home or school life, etc. One must show how it supplements the factual information found in reference materials.

In one school where the library was used as a basic tool of the social studies program, the librarian led a sixth grade class in a discussion on what they could learn from fiction. The children mentioned the countryside, homes, food, costumes or clothing, schools, agriculture, industries, games and climate. Rain in the Winds and Jungle Book were shared by children in the library in connection with the class study on India, primarily to stimulate further pleasure reading in this area but also to point out some of the information one could gain from this reading.[17]

One school's attempt to broaden the base of depth studies in the social studies program, to enrich value elements and to promote better human relations and international understanding resulted in a reading program. The Great Books of the Social Studies was developed by a faculty committee with the librarian as chairman. The group attempted to select a set of books, rich in social implications and worthy to stand as fine literature over and beyond their informational content or potential usefulness in any unit. They believed all children should have the enriching benefits of these books while in elementary school because each title has some special value to contribute to their social maturing.[18]

Special collections of books and materials which stress interracial development and understanding are now receiving attention at the elementary level and should be in evidence in all libraries. Titles such as Lift Every Voice; A Glorious Age--Africa; People

Curriculum Support

and their Actions in Social Roles; International Library of Negro Life and History; Four Took Freedom; along with the familiar All About Us; People are Important; Bright April; Whistle for Willie; and Jazz Country are basic. It is interesting to note that many of the children, both black and white, still express an interest in Paul Laurence Dunbar's poetry. The need for racial understanding in today's society can be aided by objective selection of materials at all levels.

Biography, too, occupies an important place in broadening interests and adding information. A more obvious help than fiction, it also will appeal to the child who is baffled or bored by straight factual writing. In one fourth-grade room which was studying trees, seeds and flowers, the teacher made an interesting connection with the biography of George Washington Carver and his interest in plant experimentation. His valuable contribution to the humanities was also stressed and a good understanding of the relationship between science and human welfare was developed.[19]

The variety in subject materials which the library affords makes its valuable contributions to the whole school curriculum. Such a collection also insures provision for independent reading as well as for large and simultaneous loans to classrooms.

Specific Curriculum Practices

Social studies. The broad program of social studies includes many areas of life. Historical and geographical concepts are taught. International, interracial and interreligious understandings are developed. Modern community life is studied from the familiar helpers to international government. The philosophy of democracy and of other ideologies is presented in order that intelligent decisions may be drawn. The elementary school library must have materials to answer questions in any or all of these fields, not only for the planned unit work but at other times as well.

When the current events clippings are brought in for room discussion, the librarian must be prepared to help the student to follow all avenues of interest which may arise; to look up the history, geography and economic background on the Suez or on Viet Nam, for instance; or to check on a point of local government which may have been disputed in the city council meeting of the previous day.

Some examples of units on the various grade levels are presented here to clarify the specific relationship of the library in the development of the social studies program.

The emphasis in fourth-grade programs, in general, is on people of other lands, an appreciation of how they live. In one school the teacher usually began by stressing books on children of other lands. The children then shared their impressions through panel reports.[20] Another teacher stated that the text was only a jumping-off place to the use of many library materials. In a system where no textbook is used in any social living unit, a teacher said, "We are completely dependent upon the library. For instance, in studying Switzerland we use fiction such as Kobi, Heidi, and Peterli and the Mountain for background reading; while for Norway, we use Viking myths and folklore."[21]

The pre-planning carried on by one group working on the Amazon country is an excellent illustration of the teacher's knowledge of the library, the children's use of materials and the librarian's cooperation. The reading ability in this room ranged from second grade to eighth and from an I.Q. of 89 to one of 154. This required a wide variety of materials and much individual planning. The teacher began the discussion by asking, "What do we know already?" The children then listed words which they needed to understand, i.e., mahogany, cacao beans, manioca, anteater. Volunteers to look these up in the

Curriculum Support

dictionary were reminded also of the three sets of encyclopedias available and where they would look for more detailed explanation. Two "detectives" were chosen to look for films, especially those on rivers. "The films are listed on orange cards in the card catalog," said one child, and then discussed the process of writing out the request slips. As a puppet show was being planned, music for Congo, Africa or South American jungles was needed. The blue catalog cards on which recordings are listed would help this group. The animals noted from previous readings were named--jaguar, snakes, sloths, etc., and one child remarked that there were some special books in the library on kinds of animals. The teacher reminded all that there were other interesting books to look for--stories for fun, geography books and folktales. One committee of slow readers was asked to check the <u>National Geographic Magazine</u> pictures.

"Try your books first," said the teacher, "read the first page and see if it makes sense to you. If there are too many words you don't understand, then try to find an easier one. Reading is just like running; some people are fast, some medium and some slow. Arithmetic is the same way. Find your own speed. We will have a quiet working time in the library of about thirty minutes and then an exchange period. You might also look for books for the library table in our room." After some further discussion on various interests, the group had a quick review on library manners. The children pointed out that "the library is a quiet place. You shouldn't talk to someone who is trying to read. You should put the book back in the right place and wait quietly at the charging desk." The teacher and the group departed for the library with the reminder, "Have a working time, a quiet time and a fun time."

Although this teacher came to the library with her group, the librarian had been alerted previously and several collections for certain special interest groups were already on tables. Some children went straight to the card catalog, others to the encyclopedia. Teacher and librarian circulated freely to guide all students.

During the listening time in the follow-up period in the room, the children gave brief reports in their own words "because if we wanted to copy the encyclopedia we could bring the book instead!" The teacher helped clarify words and pointed out significant terms. Several showed magazine pictures and others reported on possible filmstrips and movies. This latter group had learned that the call number for films was just like the call number for the books on that subject. Many books had been brought back for the library table, and the promise of a rich sharing of knowledge was foreseeable.[22]

Fifth grade children are primarily interested in the United States, both historically and geographically, as well as in the implications of modern day living.

Said one teacher, "Books which develop oral reports by students and books which provide background for teachers are checked from the library. The group uses all methods for finding everything they can. A bibliography of all references used is made and the children indicate--best, most enjoyable, most helpful. The following check list is used for perusing all materials on the room library tables: index, table of contents, picture captions and maps. The children are encouraged to evaluate which story is the most sensible or the most helpful. When reading biography, they check birth dates and differing information for concrete examples of inaccuracies. They then try to determine which book is more reliable and why. They learn the importance of accuracy and learn to examine critically."[23]

In a room where they were studying early

Curriculum Support   35

American explorers, the collective biographies were kept in the classroom and the individual ones in the library. There was a heavy demand for historical materials. A filmstrip viewer was available for previewing and for sharing in special reports. The children usually borrowed books individually except for titles which would be used by many of the boys and girls; these books went to the room. Colonial Life and Westward Expansion units followed much this same pattern. This teacher made use of good read-aloud books. Typical titles found in both situations were:[24]

Averill.	Voyages of Jacques Cartier.
Daugherty.	Landing of the Pilgrims.
Hark.	Story of the Pennsylvania Dutch.
Judson.	Benjamin Franklin.
Lawson.	Watchwords of Liberty.

One group starting their work on the New England states went to the library for instructions in searching for materials. The children were to find books on the shelves to check out for room use. The librarian discussed the card catalog, especially the subject cards. She pointed out the need to think of smaller or subtopics. To demonstrate, the librarian listed a broad subject heading, "New England States," and then listed separate subjects as suggested by the children, e.g., Maine--Stories (this called attention to fiction); Fishing (Fisheries) (this showed variation in forms). Each child was to "think about your state and list the sub-topics. Make your list and then go to the card catalog to see what you can find yourself." The teacher capitalized on the wealth of New England authors and poets and made a connection between the social studies and language arts programs by introducing poems which the children enjoyed.[25]

Reading in this area leads to books on government, maps and atlases as well as to fiction. Both historical and regional stories give good background throughout the fifth grade program. The Lois Lenski regional titles and many of the "Landmark" books are popular in this group, as are those by Wilder and Brink. One group, while studying the Middle Atlantic States, gave special attention to the United Nations and included You and the United Nations, A Garden We Planted Together and Rainbow Round the World. Commented their teacher, "I am constantly suggesting that as they wonder they should follow through with library experiences."26

A somewhat different approach was developed by a fifth grade studying transportation. They had listed questions covering the period from 1680 to 1900 and had made use of the card catalog to find answers to such points as, "what had to come before the 'horseless carriage' could be invented?" or, "why should we know about the ancient world's attempts to travel?"27

In yet another fifth grade, biographies formed the basis for a study of the American Revolution. Each student chose a biography about a person in that period and then checked in the library to determine whether or not the factual content was accurate. They wrote out their own questions prior to the search. For example, on Paul Revere: How far did he ride? How long did it take him? Were the signals from the tower really used? The group then participated by: (1) writing their own biography of the person; (2) taking the part of reporters and illustraters; (3) making transparencies; (4) debating the pros and cons of war. They wrote the Declaration of Independence in their own language! Johnny Tremain was the favorite book and the record of "John Paul Jones" the favorite listening.28

In the sixth grade there appear to be two general emphases in the social studies program: (1) the heritage from ancient civilization; and (2) the introduction of world geography and its present day implications.

Some schools approached this study through the

Curriculum Support

broad topic, Races of Man. The teachers and children planned together to gather information from all kinds of books. They discussed where they could find help and the type of materials for which to look. For their social studies notebooks, children took notes in class from other reports; learned how to make charts from materials read; included individual library reports on special interests. These reports covered such topics as papyrus, picture writing, cuneiform, the printing press, Roman law, Renaissance art, crafts and guilds, and religions. All this work was directed toward learning how people of the past help us today. Such titles as Cave of the Great Hunters, Exploring the Old World, World's Great Religions, The Truth Is One, Child's History of the World, Story of Mankind and Leonardo Da Vinci were found to be of great value in these programs. In addition, copies of Michelangelo's sculptures were exhibited as well as prints from the public library.[29]

Studies of Greece include both ancient and modern civilizations. In one room, after some teacher-pupil planning to organize the unit, the children discussed sources of information including the picture collection, story books and special reference materials. One group of children tape recorded the first chapter of Web of Traitors to create background for the rest of the class, and another group developed a pantomime from the Twelve Labors of Hercules. Industry, topography and present social conditions of modern Greece were covered by special reports.[30] Favorite Greek myths were shared in another school to coincide with the use of a filmstrip on gods and goddesses. This teacher brought in modern Greek civilization by using the encyclopedia first and then following with other kinds of books. The librarian read stories and introduced some Snedeker titles which related to the unit.[31]

Egypt is another country frequently studied in this grade, but, as one teacher suggested, "We really study all Africa, not just Egypt, because so much is happening there today." The group in this room divided the country into various areas for small group activity. The chairman of each group assigned specific topics to each child within his committee. The small groups took turns going to the library, alternating with groups working in the room with textbooks, art work, etc. The whole class went for group reference work at other times. This teacher preferred to use the material in the library where it was available to all. "It is necessary to emphasize the kinds of materials available," said this teacher. "Children still lean heavily on straight factual materials and need an introduction to filmstrips, vertical file materials and fiction books." Each group collected special books for a display which they shared with the others so that all were familiar with the entire study.[32]

Another group working in this area began with the idea that Africa is many things, and the teacher read aloud from Cowtail Switch. She also used Kintu to show how children must find courage in any land or place, as well as to demonstrate how to draw background information from fiction. She attempted to develop respect for ancient customs and stimulated special reports on the contributions of modern pioneers in Africa, using Schweitzer and Livingstone as examples. In guiding the use of books for reports, this teacher introduced the children to the book through the title page and table of contents; suggested that they choose a part that appealed to them, and look for illustrations and photographs as well as for accuracy and type of information. The group also relied on the National Geographic Index and on almanacs for supplementary information. Gift of the River and Boy of the Pyramids proved popular, as in many sixth grade rooms.[33]

A device used by one room was the adoption of a Merchant Marine ship for the year. This group planned to study ports, cargoes and routes, to understand why certain cargoes were picked up and where they would be taken. They would write letters to the

Curriculum Support

captain once a month. Maps and globes were to be used to trace the route followed. The library was used to find out about Singapore, the first port of call. The children explained that library materials would suggest good questions for their letters besides giving them background for understanding the captain's replies.

This particular room had recently had an interesting experience with the book, One God. The children had shared it aloud because of recent Jewish holidays, and the Jewish children in the room had explained the Torah and certain ceremonies to the rest of the group, because "they all wanted to know about each other."[34] This aspect of the humanities is one in which many teachers are doing fine work toward developing understandings.

The librarian in another school helped a class to begin its study of Italy. A list of items with which the children were expected to be familiar was worked out with the teacher prior to the library visit. The librarian listed these on her chart rack under "Italy Past" and "Italy Modern." The class was to look for material to use during the library period as well as for items to check out in the teacher's name. The librarian began by asking the question, "How would you find out if we have anything in the library on Italy?" The card catalog was mentioned, and one student volunteered to check the "I" drawer, while others took turns locating the books. This meant reviewing the subject and analytic cards as well as the shelf arrangement of classified, fiction and easy books. The next question posed was, "Where else besides the card catalog would you look?" The encyclopedias and the picture file were mentioned with the reminder that the headings of Italy and Rome should both be investigated. The "Tower of Pisa" was pointed out on the list and a discussion of pronunciation and the use of the unabridged dictionary followed. This class had an exciting and profitable period in their library.[35]

The variety of topics discussed by sixth-grade students is phenomenal. The Spanish Civil War, the solar system, UFO's, Foreign Aid, Smoking--good or bad--are some of the current areas of interest. A breadth in books and depth in periodicals is essential for this, but as one young bibliophile commented, "This library is so big you can always find materials on some topic in which you're interested."

It is apparent that in any area of the social studies program the broadest use of library materials and the cooperative planning of teacher and librarian are imperative if the topics are to be taught adequately.

Science. Science is receiving much emphasis in all grades of the elementary school and children are vitally interested in its many different aspects. There was scarcely a teacher in any school or grade visited who did not remark that she was most grateful for the library collection of books to provide her own background in a subject that is moving with such rapidity, and in which children's acceptance and comprehension often far exceed the ordinary elementary teacher's.

Nature study has always been popular. Birds, animals, plants and rocks continue to excite the curiosity of the youngest through the years. Astronomy and simple experiments in chemistry and physics are also of interest, while more recently nuclear- and astrophysics are receiving special attention. Satellites, rockets and jets are currently in ascendency. The series of Apollo flights has promulgated a completely new educational experience in this area. Television and magazine articles have made it possible for students and teachers to participate in a personal immediate experience never before a part of their learning or teaching. Such experience will become even more a part of the overall curriculum as science pushes toward new frontiers. Utilizing these programs to sharpen new interests is an important part of today's teaching in science although they sometimes provide super-

Curriculum Support   41

ficial knowledge which needs to be filled in. As one
teacher expressed it, "The teacher needs to emphasize
the who, when, what and where which underlies the
radio and television programs."[36] The elementary
school library provides adequate information for these
questions and needs.

Topics in science are not limited to any one
grade, and the librarian must make available books
on all reading levels in all of the science subjects.
Frequently, schools do not require any specific science
textbook and the work must be done entirely from library
books. One teacher emphasized individual interests
more than group study and used the library for
variety from year to year. In another community a
committee worked in the library and brought collections
of books on units to the room.

In one sixth-grade room the teacher was particularly
interested in science and drew heavily on
public and university libraries as well as on the school
library for background information. The class made
regular use of the school library and had liberty in its
selection of materials although the teacher made recommendations.
He encouraged the children to find
books of interest to the class and did not feel the need
of a room library. He used basic books for curriculum
outlines but "pursued new tangents on the old materials."
Basic texts too often are "busy work for the top group"
and, therefore, they are encouraged to expand into
special topics such as Isaac Newton, Galileo's theory,
etc. Probing is encouraged by "let's go to the encyclopedia
for a condensed version of all the basic facts
and then gather detailed information on certain facts
from other sources." This teacher noted that the interest
in pure science was stronger in the sixth grade in
this school while the interest in the scientists and biography
in general was more evident in the fifth.[37]

Fourth-graders seem to be more interested
in nature study than are fifth- or sixth-grade children.

In one library a fourth grade group was working on "The Earth We Live On." Each child had a large manila envelope on which was written the questions for which he was responsible. When he had found the answers, he slipped them in the envelope. On the back he noted the sources used and the pages. When this reference period was over, the children compared answers and were thus able to dispute or to prove a point in discussion. Before starting this work, the teacher had asked the group where in a book one would find out if it had any information of use to him. A variety of references was examined with guidance by the librarian and the teacher. This particular class followed broad interest patterns throughout the year, such as space travel, animals and plants, homes, races of people, and it made regular use of the library at all times.[38]

Reading about insects was stimulated in a fourth-grade group by the visit of a praying mantis. Each child reported information which he thought no one else could find about an insect. The praying mantis itself ended up in a cage in the library because "everyone in school could share her there." The display also included Strange Visitor and other books such as Insect World, Junior Book of Insects, Insects, and First Book of Bugs. as well as a story written by one of the children.[39]

A Nature Trail of particular interest to fourth-graders has recently been developed in another system. The guide for use of the trail included a sheet prepared by the librarians on sources for films, filmstrips, slides, recordings and books, and the note "your school librarian will work with you in preparing a list of materials suitable for your use in connection with the nature trail. Please seek her help for both personal and pupil information and enrichment reading."[40]

Beginning a new unit on Manufacturing, a

Curriculum Support 43

fourth-grade class approached it through "I wonder" questions: How coal is formed? How steel is made? About mine shafts and cave-ins? Discussion in the library was guided along these lines. How would you use the card catalog to find answers? What do you look under? (Natural Resources, Mining, Machines Steel). What will you need to find the book? The filmstrip? (call number, author, title). What other kinds of books might be helpful? Would tall tales be good? (John Henry, Joe Mageroc). Biography? Picture Materials? (Paddle-to-the-Sea). And so the children were led to explore on their own the various tools and materials in the library which had relevancy to their own interests.[41]

One fifth-grade group had prepared science notebooks on their individual interests. One boy's was on "Electricity on Earth and in Space." He had listed seventeen books. He included the latest information available and also his own ingenious idea of how electricity might be created in space. In this group, the teacher stressed creativity and emphasized, "One book is not an authority because of human fallibility, but it must be studied and compared with others."[42]

Astronomy is popular in many schools. One sixth grade combined a map of the constellations with Greek and Roman myths and their work in Ancient Civilizations.[43] In a fifth grade room This Way to the Stars and Miss Pickerell Goes to Mars were both being enjoyed out loud. The entire class was studying the seasons and the moon. Posters combined general information on astronomy with special information on the satellites.[44]

The solar system was a topic in another room where the teacher conducted a discussion on "How do you go about using library tools and books?" Encyclopedias were examined and attention called to the volume guide, the big topic guides and the index. These are "easy to use, topical and you do not have

to read a whole book. The card catalog is the place
to look for 'Sun' or other topics. You should know
the location of the 500's or science books in the library. The unabridged dictionary gives definitions,
spelling, pronunciation and short bits of information.
When using books, check the index in the back of the
book. Check against what you already have. Check
the stories in Titles I've Heard About. Skim the pages
till you find what you want after checking the contents.
Look at all the science books in your area." This
teacher's concluding statement is of special significance.
"This kind of program simply cannot be carried out
without a good school library program."[45]

One sixth-grade room was filled with pictures
in all areas of science--Mars, rockets and the Antarctic. A chart showing the relationship of atmosphere
stratosphere, ionosphere and interplanetary space to
earth was posted next to the list of "things we want
to learn about space" and "words we want to understand." Said the teacher, "The library is a necessity
here and particularly so with the gifted. It is used
by committees for detailed studies and for regular
research periods."

With the present emphasis on science education
and on opportunities for the gifted, it would appear
that in this field alone the elementary school library
can readily justify its existence and should expand its
services.

Other curriculum areas. Curricula in health
and safety, art and music, as well as in the basic
study of arithmetic may be strengthened through library materials. One advanced sixth-grade group, for
example, was working individually on the general topic
of how to help prevent the spread of disease. The
study included physiology, food, communicable diseases,
scientists and superstitions. Each child kept a bibliography and learned how to take notes so that he could
check back for cross references as well as dip in for

Curriculum Support   45

information. There was much free reading in the
room and in the library. Pamphlets, vertical file
materials, biographies, encyclopedias, science and
superstition books were scrutinized. The group discovered that "almost everything comes from individual
books." They tied in superstitions and magic with
their study in cultural heritage by reading Batchelor's
Superstitious? Here's Why! They grew molds and
bacteria to prove what they were reading on penicillin,
and enjoyed the book Yellow Magic. Exploration down
by-paths of interest was encouraged, and it led to the
exciting use of a multitude of library materials, including Microbes at Work, Modern Medical Discoveries,
Bright Design, and Soldier Doctor.[46]

  In another school system a group was preparing
booklets on such varied topics as: Bacteria--Harmful
and Helpful; Punishments of Long Ago; What Causes
Freckles; Benjamin Franklin--A Man to Remember.
This group drew heavily on the library's vertical file.
"In studying systems of the body," one teacher commented, "much of the material is not geared to children. The teacher must interpret and read to them."
This teacher uses the opaque projector to show the
illustrations from the books while explaining the diagrams. Biographies of Florence Nightingale, the
Mayo brothers, Louis Pasteur and Clara Barton, or
Famous Men of Medicine by Chandler provide helpful
materials for these health units.[47]

  Safety, fire and conservation units are frequently dependent on the library's vertical file and
audio-visual collection for current information. One
teacher pointed out, "Minn of the Mississippi and
Paddle-to-the-Sea are among the most helpful read-
aloud books I have found for water and conservation
units.[48]

  Art and music material is generally tied in
with the social studies units, but in some schools
stress is laid on art and music appreciation. In
either case, the library collection of biographies of

famous musicians and artists and its books on paintings, art collections and orchestral instruments are important aids. These may include such titles as: Goya, Mozart, Ludwig Beethoven and The Chiming Bells, Sing for America, Child's History of Art, Famous Paintings, Story of Painting for Young People, First Book of Music, Tune Up or Picture Book of Musical Instruments.

Attention should be called to the special interest which fifth- and sixth-grade boys and girls have exhibited in Hogben's Wonderful World of Mathematics. Its stunning illustrations and clear explanations have appealed to the intermediate children far beyond the expectation of many librarians. The new math has stimulated increased use in the library. In one sixth grade the following "Research Topics for Math" were suggested:

1. The scratch method of checking subtraction.

2. How is an abacus used for multiplication?

3. How is a slide rule used?

4. What is lattice multiplication?

5. How did the Egyptians multiply?

6. The role of geometry in art, in architecture.

7. What are some advantages of the metric system of measures?

8. Construct an abacus for base twelve.

9. Leonardo of Pisa and his contributions to mathematics.

Curriculum Support   47

All topics were to be covered as fully as possible.
A bibliography was required; also a title page. Class
discussion added to the topics suggested and the librarian really made use of the entire library collection of materials to help satisfy the curiosity of the
elementary student and his eagerness to expand his
knowledge.[49]

Services to Special Groups

The elementary school library has a responsibility for special services which ensure total education for all of the children. The materials and the
program must be considered in light of the needs of
the slow learner, the gifted, the handicapped (emotionally or mentally or physically) and the culturally
deprived.

Gifted children. The library is one of the
most important teachers of the gifted child. This
was the conclusion reached at one institute on the
gifted child,[50] and may prove to be one of the strong-
est justifications for a full school library program in
every elementary school.

Gifted readers need variety and depth in their
reading material. The children with special interests
and abilities in science need more detailed, more
advanced information. Such material is easily available through a good library collection where it may
be distributed judiciously by a trained librarian who
is aware of the individual needs of her clientele. The
library presents the opportunity for the child to explore on his own. It offers a place and time in the
school program for face to face conversation about
books. It allows for the wide reading necessary
where textbooks are inadequate. In school after school
the teachers' comments substantiated this. "Gifted
children must have time to read and materials to
explore. It is important to keep them busy construct-
ively; not to let them become bored. The library is

the facility which provides this service."

A sixth-grade group of gifted children in one system regularly used the junior high library in order to have access to more advanced materials. There were many books in the room of the caliber of Wells' Outline of History, Hogben's Wonderful World of Mathematics, The Iliad, The Odyssey, and Moby Dick, as well as two recent editions of encyclopedias. The reading level for this group ranged from tenth to twelfth grade. This group was preparing to make individual studies in various fields of science, to conduct experiments and to make reports to the class. Subjects such as magnets, crystals, inks, electricity, steam and jet propulsion were chosen for exploration. During the group preparation, prior to the library visit, the teacher emphasized the need for using multiple sources. Encyclopedias "word it differently but contain the same general information. You must use books and magazine articles with specific and detailed information on your subject. When you are starting to experiment, it is an advantage to have a book to guide you." It was agreed that it is important to use books because "we need to know what is in them and references are important in order to answer questions from other members of the class. Bibliographies for reports are also necessary because you share many library books with many people." The teacher noted here that the tendency to verbatim copying is still evident and that gifted children are as much in need of guidance as are others.

The majority of the recreational reading of these children is a direct outgrowth of their room interests, and they consider their science reading to be recreational reading. Although they make much greater use of reference materials, these children are otherwise about equal in their recreational interests to the usual sixth-grader. The librarian commenting on their work habits said, "These children go after a subject like life and dealth. Their power of concentration is tremendous." The class as a whole went to the library

Curriculum Support   49

twice a week and the teacher invariably followed up
the experience in the room after each period. The
daily use of library facilities by individuals and committees was incessant.[51]

In one system a five-year study was conducted
to determine whether gifted children, i.e., those
with an I.Q. of 120 or higher, would develop most
from completely segregated, partially segregated or
regular but enriched classroom programs. The direct-
or of special services, who was in charge of this
program, made some interesting comments relating
reading to library services. She indicated that at
present, academically speaking, there is no significant
difference in the grouping. The partially segregated
groups seem to be making the most progress, but
possibly that is because they have had to establish
better work habits and because they are stimulated by
two classroom teachers. The library is particularly
important in this work because: (1) it presents materials on the actual level of interests; (2) it contributes
special articles; (3) it extends information and pleasure
reading. In addition, the director pointed out, this
study has called attention to the difference of levels
in children in all classrooms and indicated the great
need for variety in teaching materials and methods.
The library makes a vital contribution, therefore, to
all children who read eagerly and widely. Because the
elementary school library is so organized within the
school that it reaches all children, it has become one
of the most important single influences in the public
school today. The teachers of these gifted children
indicated that while wide reading was being carried
on in their classrooms, more interest is shown in
factual material than in fiction. Accordingly, much
of the librarian's effort, beyond the task of enriching
the broader curriculum needs of this group, has been
directed toward developing recreational reading.[52]

In this same system a group of partially
segregated children in a fifth-grade room, i.e., ten
children who meet with a special teacher for one-half

day three times a week, used no textbooks at all
and were completely dependent upon the library for
materials. The librarian had given instruction in
the use of the card catalog and reference tools and
had also introduced them to the public library. She
occasionally conducted special discussions on groups
of books, such as biographies, to discuss standards,
style of writing and information available. Their
teacher commented, "I am definitely in favor of using
the library for gifted children; turn them loose and
let them go to town. We go to the library whenever
we need to, as groups or individuals. It is important
for children to know all library sources." This
teacher was interested particularly in human relationships and understandings and effectively used the panel
discussion device to present, through books, other
people's thinking on these problems. Each child in
the panel read one of the following books: The Hundred
Dresses, Bright April, Twenty and Ten, Jareb, All of
a Kind Family. Five questions were planned to show:
(1) the kind of person the main character was; (2)
the family background; (3) how the other characters
treated him; (4) his reactions; (5) evaluation. Every
child on the panel discussed the first question in relation to his book, and then the second and so on. The
panel members then made a general summarization of
all the books. This was followed by the class reactions. Said the teacher, "Human relations can be seen
and understood by this group more clearly than by
regular fifth-grade groups. These children are reading
from a list of fifty books, chosen by the librarian,
to learn about human beings. They are encouraged
to read not only to see how the characters react but
also to look for honesty and integrity on the part of
the author."

  This group was also learning French and in
their study used Saint Exupéry's The Little Prince with
the French record as well as other French background
books of literary merit. Again, in their special unit
on Russia, they made use of library materials,

Curriculum Support

especially articles and magazines on current problems.[53] It was evident that this type of program, where the group worked on basic skills in the regular classroom and then were free to explore other areas of interest under the guidance of a special teacher, stimulated heavy use of many library materials.

The use of paperbacks with sixth-graders in an advanced reading group promoted a thoughtful introduction of adult titles such as <u>I Remember Mama,</u> <u>Lost Horizons, You Can't Take It With You.</u> The children "discovered" these books in the library and in turn talked about them with their parents. The guidance of the librarian in preparing the more mature readers for this leap and the inclusion of the parents in the planning are significant aspects of in-service to the gifted.[54]

<u>Slow learners.</u> The librarian in the elementary school not only helps the gifted, she is of equal assistance in providing special reading material to those at the slower end of the learning scale. A remedial reading specialist stated that the librarian greatly aided in her program. "She looks for books for easy reading with high interest levels. She gives individual guidance to the slow learner. She pays special attention to co-ordinating the curriculum materials for the slower reader with the subject interests which others in the room are studying."[55]

Assistance to the slow or mentally retarded child requires much patience on the part of the librarian and a more subtle approach than that used with the gifted reader. Lists of material of high interest and low vocabulary are in constant use by both teacher and librarian, and complete knowledge of the library collection is required. This is true especially where teachers rely more heavily on library books than they do on standard texts for the slow reading groups.

In one school the librarian explained that she worked most carefully with slow readers in order to develop their confidence. In this particular school, where this is a problem of some extent, the librarian deliberately placed many "easy" books in the regular classified sections so that she might give "something you'll enjoy" to a slow reader in the intermediate grades without hurting his pride.[56]

"The slow child may be stimulated without discrimination by comrades, in selection of books through the library," stated one teacher. While her cohort added, "I try to keep the slower readers in library books while larger groups are using regular readers. Then everybody in the room is reading at once. With slower children it's easier to bring many library materials, particularly easy books, to the room. This is helpful for individual guidance. They enjoy finding their own books and not just using the ones the teacher specifically gives them."[57]

In working with very slow groups the elementary school library is used extensively by the special teachers. Emphasis is placed on teaching about practical matters, and books on food, clothing, shelter, newspapers, health and safety are checked out in quantity. Portions of these will probably be rewritten on three or four reading levels by the teachers, but the basic information and the pictures are essential in this teaching program. In one room where the I.Q. ranged from 50 to 75, the teachers explained that the boys and girls were enjoying book reports. They had read and reported on Lazy Liza Lizard, Miss Flora McFlimsey and Nils. But they particularly loved to listen to stories, and the librarian and the teachers took turns with this program. The children "can make wonderful illustrations and remember the stories even if they can't read." They especially enjoy simple fairy stories like "Goldilocks," "Pied Piper of Hamelin," "Peter Rabbit." Several of these "non-readers" of about fifth-grade age help in the library by putting away easy books.[58]

Curriculum Support

In another system the educable group was segregated only part of the day and these children came to the library with their peer groups. A special library table with easy and picture book materials was always ready for them. Many easy books were available in their classrooms, and they were beginning to understand where these books came from and to ask the librarian for specific titles in their visits to the library. When the entire class was in the library, they were divided into slow and fast groups so that the teacher might work with one group while the librarian helped the other. These slow readers had definite favorites, such as the Blaze and Flip stories. Appreciation of the pictures and, thereby, comprehension of the story was the general method of approach.[59]

The librarian can be of assistance also to the teachers working with the trainable group, i.e., I.Q. below 50. This group must learn how to read some basic information for their protection. Filmstrips borrowed from the library are useful. The teacher reads while the children participate through picture recognition. Again, picture books which have stories about everyday experiences, tying in with the field trip to the fire station or the grocery store, situations with which these children must become familiar, make a valuable contribution. Library story hours are prime favorites with these groups.[60] In non-segregated groups it is most important to make available something which the slow child can use as his contribution in the same areas as his classmates.

It is good for trainable children to be in a situation where other children come to work informally. As one principal indicated, "This school may be the only place where they will get real citizenship training. They must be literate for survival." The library permits the use of many types of media to help in verbalization. Filmstrips, which can be viewed over and over again or on an individualized basis to satisfy reading and storytelling needs, and the overhead projector, which intrigues the youngster by light and reflection and bolsters self image and esteem, place the media center in a prominent teaching role.[61]

A teacher checks out special airplane books for a second grade problem child; a challenge group which delights in simple biographies of explorers and pioneers finds satisfaction in the library; a nine year old boy in the first grade becomes a library helper and learns to "read pictures" --these are examples which may be duplicated in every elementary school where there is a library and a trained librarian to help the slow learner.

<u>Physically handicapped children.</u> The elementary school librarian has many opportunities to work with physically handicapped children in her school community, both through the home and the school. Close cooperation with the visiting teacher makes it possible for homebound children to have access to the library books which they need in order to pursue their regular classroom studies as well as for pleasure.

Children who are able to attend school despite their physical handicaps are encouraged to participate as far as possible in the entire school program. During part of the day they may attend special classes designed to assist them in learning to overcome their particular difficulties, but most of the time is spent with their peers. The services of the librarian are available to both groups. Transparencies have been valuable with cerebral palsy groups, as have talking books and large print books.

In one school where a wing was provided for physically handicapped children, the boys and girls participated in regular class functions including the library program. It was common for a child to come scooting into the library in his wheelchair or on crutches to do reference work, to read for pleasure,

Curriculum Support

or to help the librarian card books or sort cards. When it was impossible for the children to come to the library, the librarian supplemented the work of the therapists with special book collections.[62]

In several of the schools visited, work was being done in sight-saving classes as well as with totally blind children. In all situations, the librarian included special collections of books with large print and books in Braille. The blind children in one school ranged from kindergarten through the fourth grade and came to the library with their regular classes. There were two Braille collections available, one of easy or picture books and the other of intermediate books. One mother, who was especially interested in this field, converted many favorite titles into Braille. She had also written the text above the Braille to facilitate adult guidance in reading. Both the librarian and the teachers working with these children were taking lessons in Braille in order to be of more assistance to the children. These boys and girls are all learning how to use Braille machines and styluses and are able to begin to search and make notes.[63]

<u>Culturally disadvantaged.</u> There is a special emphasis today on service to the students who come from homes where there is little material or cultural background, where the adults in the community pay scant attention to the needs of the young, where school itself is a "sometime thing." The multi-media center plays a most strategic role in the life of these youngsters from pre-school onward. The following statement of philosophy from one demonstration school epitomizes not only the total media concept but the absolutely necessary relationship between the media itself and the level of service demanded by this group.[64]

"Our library qualifies truly as a learning resources center. Information is housed in many different containers. The usage of varied media is a fact.

"The library with all its available resources, human and materials, exists to further the objectives of this school. Since our school is completely organized into non-graded and team teaching units, we consider the library team's existence is justified through service to the other teams.

"Our library has succeeded or failed solely on the ratings of worth given it by pupils and teachers. If we do not have what they are seeking and are not answering their pleas for help individually or as a group we have failed. It is only on how wisely and well these materials are selected and circulated to meet our unique needs that we ask to be evaluated. We have a single-minded objective to serve our school as it needs our services.

"Incidentally, teachers and pupils cannot always know or anticipate their own needs. Therefore, we must not wait to be called upon but volunteer. This is possible only because of our own awareness of the entire and individual instructional program."

Such a statement demonstrates that librarians can help all children discover that "the round peg doesn't fit in the square hole."

In all these areas then--for the mentally retarded, the gifted, the physically handicapped, the disadvantaged--the elementary school librarian, through her knowledge of curriculum needs and reading abilities, makes a careful selection of media and contributes effectively to the education of these children.

References

1. College Hill School, Evanston, Illinois.
2. Munsey Park School, Manhasset, New York.
3. Ibid.
4. Whitehall School, Jackson, Tennessee.

Curriculum Support   57

5. Plandome Road School, Manhasset, New York.
6. Oakton School, Evanston, Illinois.
7. Plandome Road School, Manhasset, New York.
8. Bush School, Jamestown, New York.
9. Longfellow School, Royal Oak, Michigan.
10. Casis School, Austin, Texas.
11. Plandome Road School, Manhasset, New York.
12. Meadows School, Fulton County, Georgia.
13. Mitchell School, Fulton County, Georgia.
14. Ibid.
15. Ibid.
16. Munsey Park School, Manhasset, New York.
17. Longfellow School, Royal Oak, Michigan.
18. Casis School, Austin, Texas.
19. Plandome Road School, Manhasset, New York.
20. Casis School, Austin, Texas.
21. Oakleigh School, Baltimore County, Maryland.
22. Craven School, Austin, Texas.
23. Casis School, Austin, Texas.
24. Ibid.
25. Fairmount School, Jamestown, New York.
26. Sternberger School, Greensboro, North Carolina.
27. Plandome Road School, Manhasset, New York.
28. Dodson School, Fulton County, Georgia.
29. Plandome Road School, Manhasset, New York.
30. Casis School, Austin, Texas.
31. Cossitt School, LaGrange, Illinois.
32. Brooks School, Greensboro, North Carolina.

33. Fairmount School, Jamestown, New York.
34. Casis School, Austin, Texas.
35. Mitchell School, Fulton County, Georgia.
36. Rogers School, Jamestown, New York.
37. Davis School, Evanston, Illinois.
38. Oakleigh School, Baltimore County, Maryland.
39. Brooks School, Greensboro, North Carolina.
40. Greensboro, North Carolina.
41. Chisholm Trail School, Wichita, Kansas.
42. Orrington School, Evanston, Illinois.
43. Loch Raven School, Baltimore County, Maryland.
44. Ibid.
45. Oakleigh School, Baltimore County, Maryland.
46. Campfield School, Baltimore County, Maryland.
47. Plandome Road School, Manhasset, New York.
48. Casis School, Austin, Texas.
49. Oak Knoll School, Fulton County, Georgia.
50. Casis School, Austin, Texas.
51. Kiser Junior High School, Greensboro, North Carolina.
52. Evanston, Illinois.
53. Lincoln School, Evanston, Illinois.
54. Casis School, Austin, Texas.
55. Parkview School, Jackson, Tennessee.
56. Lincoln School, Jackson, Tennessee.
57. Bush School, Jamestown, New York.
58. Rogers School, Jamestown, New York.
59. McIver School, Greensboro, North Carolina.

Curriculum Support

60. Jones School, Greensboro, North Carolina.
61. Lawsonville Avenue School, Reidsville, North Carolina.
62. Casis School, Austin, Texas.
63. Davis School, Evanston, Illinois.
64. Lawsonville Avenue School, Reidsville, North Carolina.

Chapter III

Reading Guidance in the Middle Grades

> Reading is a high art because it is a
> generous art, like listening. It is to
> writing as listening is to speaking,
> and the educated person does all four
> things more or less equally well.
>
> Mark Van Doren[1]

The second major phase of the elementary school library program, paralleling the work in curriculum enrichment, is reading guidance. Interpreted broadly, this includes guidance on the part of both teacher and librarian in helping the child to choose books on his own reading level and in his own special interests; to develop standards for appreciation of good books; and, to interpret the joys in reading for pleasure. It is rather absurd to attempt to establish an arbitrary division of reading guidance between the librarian and the teacher, for the program is a cooperative effort. Yet there are certain phases of the program for which the librarian seems to be well suited, and other areas for which the teacher should be primarily responsible. At the risk of some duplication, an attempt will be made here to indicate both approaches. The presentation of actual situations in elementary schools will serve to illustrate: (1) programs developed by librarians in the field of reading guidance and appreciation; (2) methods and plans used by teachers for developing these same areas in classroom work; (3) experiences in poetry appreciation and creative expression; (4) reading records and book sharing devices.

It is not the responsibility of the school librarian to teach the techniques and skills of reading, although she must have some understanding of the general psychology of reading. It is her responsibility, however, to provide books which will expand the reading interest and vocabularies of the students and will guide them into the delights of reading for enjoyment as well as information, and to stimulate interest through book talks, story hours and other devices. It is the purpose of the school library to surround boys and girls with books representing the finest in literature as well as books that will serve as stepping stones to these; with books which provide the "best" for the beginning readers and for the advanced readers; with books that will present adventure or humor, mystery or sports, fairytales or romance, sad stories or family stories, travel or lives of famous people--whatever the particular interest may be at a particular time.

Children have moods and desires as do adults, and what may be perfectly satisfactory one day is anything but a "good book" the next day. The alert librarian watches for these changes and knows her collection adequately so that she may guide the reader to new books as the new interests appear.

> Children are not as a rule aware that they are growing as people when they are having a good time with books and that is, of course, the reason why they grow so freely. Complete abandonment to the pleasure of whatever kind of reading most appeals to them opens the way for deep and lasting impressions to settle into mind and heart. Once they can read fluently ... all they need is a little help in finding good solid satisfying books that fit in with their strongest interests and they will do the rest.[2]

Library Program

The librarian plans her work from two broad bases: (1) individual guidance, and (2) group guidance. She accomplishes this by: (1) supplying materials for

teacher and classroom use; (2) by suggesting books to
the individual child for home or outside reading; (3)
by conducting a library program to develop literary
appreciation through storytelling, attractive exhibits
and other devices; (4) by searching for the recordings,
films, etc., incorporating the best techniques of storytelling and the most accurate portrayals of book plots
and characters.

    Elementary school librarians are aware of the
need to develop interest in reading for pleasure and
in wide reading, and they employ a variety of methods
to achieve this. Much of this work is done with class
groups in the library. Part of the period may be
spent in individual browsing and reading and in choosing
books to take home, and part may be devoted to various
forms of group sharing which are planned to stimulate
reading for depth and breadth of information as well as
enjoyment.

    <u>Individual guidance</u>. During the browsing period,
the librarian has an excellent opportunity to carry on
individual reading guidance. To do this she must know
the reading ability of each child, and especially the
ability of slow or accelerated readers. She is dependent upon the teachers for lists of pupils and their reading levels, or upon the principal for the reading scores
available through the testing program. Her knowledge
of the collection, correlated with the above information,
makes individual guidance possible. Such guidance is
the special province of the librarian, since it is impossible for the classroom teachers to keep up with all
the new materials in all grade levels which might be
useful at various times with their students.

    It is important, too, that this individual inter-
est of the librarian be felt by the child. It helps him
to achieve satisfaction in his reading and, therefore,
pleasure. For example, during his library period,
J---, a slow fourth-grade reader, was trying to read
a book which was evidently too difficult for him. The
librarian, sensing his unhappiness, helped him find a

cub scout story with action, adventure and fairly large print. The next day he was back, bubbling over with delight, to tell the librarian that he came to school early that morning just to read his book and had read the first chapter all the way through! A sense of satisfaction was achieved coupled with an acceptance of the fact that the librarian could help him find "good stories."[3] This is the rapport that every elementary school librarian should strive to develop with the boys and girls in her school.

One librarian made use of her own hobby, a superb collection of dolls from many countries and illustrating many book characters, to help so-called non-readers. Bringing an Eskimo boy doll to school, she suggested to a fourth-grade lad that he read Panuck, and, if he enjoyed it enough to make an oral report to the class, he might use the doll as an illustration. The report was a surprise to the teacher as well as to the class, with the more important result that the boy borrowed a book every week thereafter! The same technique worked successfully with a sixth-grade girl and Miss Hickory.[4]

Capitalizing on the child's hobby brings equally good results. One librarian discovered that a fourth-grade lad collected antiques, especially guns. He read many magazines to look for the advertisements, and, as he explained, "I need to read a great deal on American History because it helps me know more about things. The Matchlock Gun is one of my favorites." A display of his collection, incidentally, made good newspaper publicity for the children's room of the public library during Book Week.[5]

Children often make a confidante of the librarian. In one school two children talked to the librarian about their problems; one was a step-child, the other, a younger brother. The librarian casually suggested reading Daringer's Stepsister Sally and Beim's Kid Brother to help them accept the fact that other children had similar problems.[6] Estes' The Hundred Dresses and De Angeli's Door in the Wall are also examples of stories which librarians in many places have found successful in developing attitudes of sympathy and understanding, or in demonstrating that physical handicaps may be overcome.[7]

Group guidance. Guidance through group participation demands careful planning. There must be variety of program. The browsing period should be meaningful and should provide opportunity for librarian and children to share books.

Story hours continue to be as popular in fourth, fifth and sixth grades as in the primary groups. This presents an opportunity for the librarian to share fairy tales and folklore; to tell some of the great myths and legends which are so rich in description, so important to an understanding of our culture, and of great interest to this age of hero worshippers. Beowulf, King Arthur, Robin Hood are favorites everywhere. The excellent recordings of the Newbery Award books, e.g., Wheel on the School, of children's classics, e.g., Treasure Island, and of modern favorites, e.g., The Singing Tree, are spell binders for story time, as well as good introductions to the books. Displays, book marks and special book talks such as those on the Newbery and Caldecott books are also a part of the librarian's program to equate appreciation and pleasure in reading. Many of the Newbery award books are particularly suitable for reading aloud. They need to be savored slowly and not gulped in one sitting for they are the type of story which often needs special presentation by one who already has an appreciation for them.

Displays of new books with short reviews of outstanding titles are always stimulating to further reading. One librarian introduced Bowman's Mike Fink by by reading from the jacket and a part of the first chapter and showing the illustrations. This led to a discussion of tall tales of all kinds and presented an opportunity to mention other exciting books.[8] Many li-

brarians ask the children to share their books when
the group is in the library. One librarian asked a
fourth grade how many had visited a new land that
week; another time, how many had made a new friend.[9]
In another school, since it was Hallowe'en, the librarian asked how many had read a spook story. This
technique encourages all children to participate. It
stimulates variety in reading. Frequently, a child will
add, "Frank likes this kind of book too," and Frank,
or Mary, will have found another story he wants to
read.

    Book discussions in the library help children
to learn to ask for books by title, to recommend books
to each other, to point out the values in "good" stories.
One librarian posed the question, "How do we choose
which of our books are best, or which one we would
like to take out?" The children suggested such things
as, "try a good sample before checking out"; "read
the book review blurb if it's pasted in the book"; "know
what authors wrote good books"; "look at some of the
chapters and a few pages"; "look for your special subject"; "read three pages at first or read the middle
chapter"; "check on whom the book is about, if it's
biography"; "if people talk about them, it sounds good";
"look for a catchy title."[10] Obviously some of these
were quick tricks; others, thoughtful procedures, but
the discussion itself did lead to more careful choices
in the future.

    Book discussion groups are encouraged at all
levels in many schools. These often revolve around
suggested reading lists prepared by school committees,
although they may also be chosen by student groups
or result from spontaneous types of interest. One
room divided itself into inner and outer circles for a
discussion in the library. The outer circle watched,
listened, criticized and questioned the discussion presented by the inner circle. Pertinent comments were
made. Generally the children conduct these sessions
themselves. Books such as <u>Incredible Journey</u>, <u>Winter
Days</u>, <u>Mocassin Trail</u>, Mr. <u>Justice Holmes</u> have been
used successfully.[11]

Emphasis on a character trait of significance is another approach. Individuals in one group shared Amos Fortune, Carry on Mr. Bowditch, Wonderful World of Math, Digging into Yesterday, Wind in the Willows and Rabbit Hill. The participants indicated that factual books could be shared because objects also have characteristics and as one child insisted, "the past had its character."[12]

Literature in depth, that is, discussion resulting from one book such as Cricket in Times Square is also exciting. This title led to a study of the author, films on New York City, the making of a cricket cage and an impressive study on the habits of crickets!

During Book Week, when many new books were on display, an introduction of new titles to fifth- and sixth-graders was combined with a lesson on making a booklist for future reading. The librarian shared six new books and then presented the idea of an individual reading list by discussing the value and fun in choosing one's own books from those on display. A large sample chart, "Books I Want to Read," was made, and included the books reviewed with author first and correct information noted. The librarian continued by explaining the reason for having the author's last name first, reminding them that the "title page is the best place to find the author's name," and suggesting that they might star the books that "look good for social studies, to help your teachers."[13]

A shelf for "Junior Reviewers" is a feature in one library. Fifth and sixth graders, who are interested in reading new books and reviewing them for the city newspaper, are invited to browse there. In writing the review they must remember "what for, for whom, what to tell and the bibliographic citation."[14]

Sixth-graders continue to enjoy writing letters to authors, but teachers are stressing that there should be a reason for writing. Have you read the book? What do you know about the author? In one school the film Lively Art of the Picture Book was shared.

The librarian followed this with a discussion of favorite books in the classroom--the boys and girls really had to be prepared to defend their books. Illustrators are equally popular and discussions of techniques and why pictures can "make" a book are lively sessions. Breadth in reading is the chief emphasis of both teacher and librarian.[15]

     Much interest has been aroused of late in the classics--partly due to magazine articles and partly to a revival through television programs. Parents are interested in having their children read the classics, even though neither parents nor children are always sure of what constitutes a children's classic. Too often adults remember only the titles connected with high school literature classes or have a vague recollection of some book read to them in their childhood, which, in all probability, is no longer in print. Many elementary school librarians have made a special effort to follow up television presentations. The children are introduced to the original story or book and become aware of its literary value and the pleasure in reading the whole story. Librarians have attempted to familiarize parents with the fine children's books presently available and the richly illustrated editions of old favorites. In one Library Club the children began to discuss the word classic. It soon became apparent to the librarian that the boys and girls did not know what it meant. They talked about favorite stories which children had enjoyed for many years, trying to understand why they had remained popular. Then they decided they would choose six to share with the school--<u>Peter Pan,</u> <u>Tom Sawyer,</u> <u>Alice in Wonderland,</u> <u>Treasure Island,</u> <u>Robinson Crusoe,</u> <u>Robin Hood.</u> In the skit presented at a school assembly during Book Week, a child, who thought books were sissy, was visited by characters from these books and discovered new friends and adventures. The narrator, in introducing the play, explained that these were especially good books for family sharing. Ever since the assembly, the books have been in circulation, and a careful check by the librarian has revealed that they definitely are being read and enjoyed.[16]

Book games, quizzes and puzzles, many of them inspired by What Book Is That? (Harshaw and McBean), are enjoyed in every library and are carried over into the classrooms. A book party game which is used effectively by one elementary school librarian is predicated on the idea that children will read because they enjoy it and because they love to share their books. A group of books on a subject which fourth-graders enjoy, or perhaps a group to which they should be introduced, is set aside in the library. During the browsing reading hours, their attention is called to this collection. A few weeks later the librarian has a "party" to see how well they can remember a story and share it. "I'm thinking of ---" begins the librarian and tells a bit about one book. The child who guesses the title then has a turn.[17] This naturally arouses great excitement and a new wave of interest in reading these books develops.

The attractive paperbacks now being published --titles which have literary worth and with attractive illustrations--will add much to the development of reading for enjoyment. It is easier to encourage the building of one's library of favorites. Likewise, it makes books available on an expendable basis in areas where children cannot afford home libraries and where the art of pleasure reading is neglected or is not known.

The opportunities for the librarian to assist individually and through groups in the widening of book horizons are manifold and form an important part of the total reading program in the school.

Classroom Programs

Closely correlated with the librarian's effort to stretch reading horizons is the teacher's program to expand reading beyond the skill and technique area into the realm of pleasure and recreation. Both teacher and librarian are interested in guiding the child to an acceptance of books as a source of information and a source of delight; to an awareness of the vicarious and enriching experiences which books bring; to an acceptance of reading as a worthwhile leisure time activity.

Teachers contrive to do this through the informal sharing of books in the classroom and through formal guidance of the children's reading activities. Such a program requires reading materials beyond the basic and supplementary text collections. In one fourth grade room, for example, the reading levels might range from first through seventh grades. One teacher expressed the problem thus: "So many people think a grade library is all that's necessary. Look at the variety of reading levels in my class, second through eight. I can't go dashing to the second grade room when I need a book on that reading level. It is important that we have a centralized collection and a librarian who can give individual assistance."[18]

Fourth grade. Reading guidance in the fourth grade is particularly significant because of the change from the primary type of reading book to the longer story. The idea of reading for pleasure receives more emphasis, and the library may serve a special purpose here. Most children want to read, say the fourth grade teachers, and the first impressions regarding reading and the library are most important. The children are affected directly by the teacher's own attitude toward the library. If the teacher herself emanates the idea that reading is fun, she can challenge their interests. Furthermore, the teacher works closely with the class when in the library. She carefully motivates their choice of books, perhaps by telling a little of the story and adding, "I wonder what happened. Please tell me the rest of the story." She attempts to help them to read, not just to look at the books. This is especially true with the slower and uninterested readers. "Careful guidance pays off in an increase of the reading ability," was a general comment. Good readers should be discouraged from reading "thin" books just to read a book. They need to discover and branch out to other interests. The teacher's knowledge of each individual is of value and must be shared with the librarian.

One teacher has a special display of books the first day of school and puts book jackets up in the classroom. She tries to create the feeling among the children that they are "coming into lots of books. Variety is a good way to ease the change from the primary program."[19] This can lead directly to increased interest in using the library.

Many teachers are conscious of the fact that readers often include only one chapter of a book. They make a special effort to encourage children to read the whole book. To assist teachers in this effort, librarians commonly check all the bibliographies in the readers against the school library collections and distribute lists of the books which are available. The teachers encourage children to read these library books and the library table in the classroom suggests such recreational reading. A propos of this, one teacher remarked, "Carolyn Haywood taught my children to read. Her stories are easy. K---, for instance, who wouldn't read a word last year, just sails through the whole book now. And Ed, a poor reader, after discovering Little Eddie has made tremendous growth."[20]

In the fourth grade teachers have found that it is important to have a silent reading period in the classroom for the purpose of reading library books. Some have it the first thing in the morning; others, right after lunch. Many teachers have a follow-up in the classroom directly after the library period. This plan is advantageous because it gives the children a "chance to really delve into their books," and gives the teacher an opportunity to observe the choice of reading material

Reading Guidance   71

more closely. It provides an opportunity for the child
to go to the library to exchange his book; it encourages
reading for pleasure; it creates a good reading atmosphere; it often leads to fruitful sharing time. It also
develops a habit which will be perpetuated through outside reading long after such classroom experiences
are ended.

          Fourth-graders thoroughly enjoy sharing their
books. Sharing encourages oral reading and audience
listening, important phases of communication. Both
teachers and students participate in the read-aloud
periods. Occasionally, a teacher will read one book
in its entirety, such as Charlotte's Web or Golden
Name Day; or she may read excerpts from different
books or even a magazine article to show that reading
may cover many areas of interest and types of materials. She tries to read books which the children
might not read by themselves. These would include
books with too high a reading level for the children
even though they are ready for them on an interest
level--folklore and legends, The Jungle Book, or
perhaps Wind in the Willows. The teacher may share
favorite fairy tales, for which children at this grade
level continue to show unabated interest.

          A read-aloud and sharing discussion that took
place in one room illustrates some of the values of
participation. The teacher was reading The White Stag
by Seredy. The use of this had stemmed originally
from a study of the Huns, a unit in a reader, and the
children had become deeply interested in the story.
After listening to part of the book, they began to discuss the story. They mentioned that part of it was
history but thought some of it was imaginative. One
girl felt that some of the "fantasy part was so lovely
you could just see them dancing in the moonlight."
This led to other books by Seredy, particularly the
Good Master, which had been introduced at another
time by the librarian. The Seredy illustrations were
particularly pleasing to the children because they were

"so unusual," "look like Hungarians," "look so real," and because "the author illustrated her own story." This statement immediately instigated a lively conversation about people who illustrate their own books, "like Holling in Minn of the Mississippi. They're usually really good books if the author and illustrator are the same."[21] This is the type of discussion for which a teacher needs a broad knowledge of children's books. It does much to stimulate reading within the group.

The children in one community spend much time becoming acquainted with the authors of their favorite books. They make reports on them and often write letters to them. A local author or illustrator frequently serves as a resource person to tell how he writes his stories; how he works with the publishers, etc. A field trip to a publishing house usually follows. Each child is expected, meanwhile, to keep a list of the books being read in order to choose his favorites for class sharing. Books from home often are brought in, and the teacher tries to help create standards for these home libraries.[22]

The development of a unit on "Books, Authors and Getting to Know Your Library" is a favorite technique in the field of reading guidance. In one room interest was stimulated by the bulletin board which was divided into three sections: (1) three large posters with poems on "Books We Are Reading"; (2) book jackets to introduce new books; (3) "Do You Know How A Book Is Made?" showing the sheet, the open signature, folded signature and cut signature for a book. A representative from a local publishing house came out to talk to the children, and a film on "How a Book Is Made" was shown. In connection with this unit, the teacher emphasized story materials and reading for fun and included an extra thirty-minute period for "fun reading" during the day. The children also discussed books written or illustrated by local people and shared their special autographed copies. A tour of the library

Reading Guidance 73

was included, and committees presented projects or reports on the types of books which they found in the library, e.g., a castle for fairy tales and the 398's; an experiment for science and the 500 books; some puppets for crafts in the 700's, etc.[23] This is obviously an excellent illustration of the close cooperative planning necessary between teacher and librarian in every phase of library work and reading guidance.

"How To Make a Book," a bulletin board in a fourth grade room far removed from the above example, was a guide to another group of children who had decided to make books. The visit of an author instigated this project, and the children determined to write their own stories or poems and "publish" them. As they proceeded to make the covers, prepare the signatures, etc., each step was illustrated on the bulletin board by examples from a publishing firm. This interest in books was particularly exciting, for at the same time the teacher was carrying on a reading program based almost entirely on the use of library books. Basal readers were used once a week if needed. The children had their own choice of reading material through a large temporary classroom library which was constantly being varied with books from the centralized collection. Many of the children were reading several books at the same time. All the different reading levels and types of materials were represented, although biography and science seemed particularly popular. The teacher was attempting to lift the sights as well as the abilities of the children, and the librarian worked closely with her. Children went to the library as the need for material arose. They usually chose a variety of books. Parents were kept fully informed and felt that the children were reading more and increasing their vocabulary through this type of reading program. Many methods of making book reports were encouraged. Said the teacher, "These children are truly more happy to keep on reading, rather than to be doing other work. It is most effective in developing reading interests and more of them are reading on the fifth-grade level. But this can work just as well with a slow group too, because it takes the penalty out of reading. Children can find stories that are important to them, for so many of the stories in readers are not really important, and there is a much broader vocabulary to explore in library books."[24]

Exploration in folklore may prove to be another stimulant in developing both reading skills and fun with reading. In one room such a study began with a class discussion of folklore people, who they are and how they came to be. This expanded into the reading of tall tales and excerpts from other collections of folklore. It culminated with the children coming to school dressed as characters from the folk tales and an original dramatization of Wicked John and the Devil. In this classroom there is need for only one formally organized reading group. All other reading is done individually with materials in the room or in the library. Although this school is in a well-to-do community, the fourth grade teacher strongly emphasized that these children "need additional library materials even though there are home libraries; perhaps, because they seem to have already acquired a deeper appreciation of literature and need broad collections on which to draw."[25]

In observing the choices of fourth-graders in many schools, it is evident that though they are still fond of fairy tales, they are strongly drawn as well to biography, to nonfiction relating to hobbies and to adventure stories for both boys and girls. Science fiction such as Miss Pickerell Goes to Mars, Space Ship Under the Apple Tree and Space Cat are extraordinarily popular at present. Teachers all agree, furthermore, that television programs have not curtailed reading by fourth-graders. In fact, many teachers capitalize on these and, as children become familiar with more people and places, they are encouraged to do wider library reading for background and to share their books and knowledge more broadly than ever.

This is the age group where exploring in books becomes highly significant.

    Fifth grade. The approach to reading guidance in the fifth grade classrooms differs with the more mature child although the interest areas are as broad and the reading levels as varied as in the fourth grade. The emphasis here appears to be on forming good reading habits, finishing a book, encouraging outside reading, formulating standards for quality and balance. "Fifth- and sixth-graders respond eagerly to reading," pointed out a teacher, "but they are prone to stick to science and mysteries. There is need for individual guidance to prevent top heaviness."[26] Another teacher expressed her belief that the fifth grade is an exciting group with which to work because of "its variety of interests that need challenging and channelling."[27] Many teachers have found an intensive reading program in the first part of this school year rather a good policy. There is much talking about books, reading aloud from books, displaying of books and stimulating of widespread reading. Considerable individual guidance is given at first, and then each child is encouraged to find his own books. The classes discuss the purposes of reading and learn how to "dip into" a book before making a final choice.

    In one situation where the teacher had two library reading groups a week, the children were grouped by interests rather than by reading level ability. Animals, famous people, science were some of the subjects selected and a variety of books was available. Another teacher, who had reading scores in her room ranging from 3.7 to 8.3, re-emphasized the importance of helping children to choose the easier books which still cover the class interests.[28] This type of guidance demands that the teacher knows the levels of books and draws heavily on the library for breadth in her classroom collections. Free reading periods in the classroom are again a recognized must, for as one teacher states, "There's nothing that makes children come up in reading like library books."[29]

At the same time, the need to form reading habits at home is emphasized with parents, and children are encouraged to use the public library for summer reading as well as leisure time reading in the school year. Teachers find they must work on developing library book reading, especially in communities where the children's leisure time is occupied with extracurricular activities. One teacher encouraged her children to test their speed in reading at home to see how much they could read and enjoy in thirty minutes a night.[30] Another teacher suggested that the children keep track of the amount of time spent reading at home. "Begin with five minutes a day and try to get up to thirty minutes a day as your goal before the end of the first semester." A letter sent to parents with the report card helped to stress this program and now, most of the boys and girls do it automatically and enjoy it.[31] Both of these efforts were planned to develop library book reading programs. There is emphasis not only on reading at home for fun but in sharing the book with other members of the family. The boy who exclaimed that he and his dad had read Gipson's Old Yeller together, and they both thought it was one of the most exciting stories they'd ever read, had a doubly rich experience with books.

The technique of reading aloud continues to be employed with this age group. One teacher, who often shares in this manner, mentioned Caddie Woodlawn as a favorite book because "it knits the group together and has such wonderful human relationships." This teacher is particularly interested in books for oral reading which are unusual and good for she believes this type of reading has particular value for the slow reader. The Wilder books too have a special purpose in this fifth-grade room. They are well loved by the girls and serve as a good bridge from family life stories to historical stories, a particularly hard jump for fifth grade girls. Another favorite read-aloud book is Call It Courage which has "a magic charm for all." Reading aloud, then, develops listening skills, helps to increase vocabulary comprehension, aids in the building of developmental values and continues to serve as an introduction to new and good books.

Opportunity for the children to share books aloud is a regular part of most fifth-grade reading programs and promotes various skills. Children learn to share without telling the whole story. They learn to use reference books such as Junior Book of Authors in order to give background information. They develop skill at reading aloud. They enjoy participation in the humorous incident, an interesting description or an unusual character. Not only does this sharing enable youngsters to learn about new books but often sufficiently intrigues the teacher to say, "Let me have it when you're through," and, added one teacher, "I enjoy them as well!"

Story telling by children is a further device for exploring books. In one school a program of story telling for fifth- and sixth-graders is a regular spring project planned by teachers and librarian. An instructor in story telling is invited to bring some of his students. The art of story telling is discussed and the students demonstrate the techniques. Several teachers follow this in their classrooms by having children choose books which they think would be of interest to boys and girls from kindergarten through second grade. They practice telling the stories before their classmates for constructive criticism. Then volunteers may tell the stories to lower grades both in the classrooms and in the library.[32] This is good experience in learning to select stories and also encourages reluctant reader participation. A similar project on a smaller scale exists in a situation where fifth- and sixth-grade children help with the first graders during the lunch hour. A special program is planned to help these girls learn how to tell stories and to choose books which will be fun to share with this younger group.[33]

In one school one part of the learning resource center was set aside for storytelling, creative dramatics, etc. A group of upper-grade youngsters had created flannel board characters to share with small groups from the kindergartens. Certain times in the library schedule were set aside for this, and teachers could suggest to youngsters that they might enjoy this activity at that time. It was a free-wheeling situation for both participants and storytellers.[34]

Realizing how much older children enjoy browsing in the picture book section, one teacher occasionally takes an extra period in the library when everyone reads "E" books for fun--teacher as well. They read individually and share together to develop general appreciation, look for beauty in illustrations and enjoy the humor. This is another helpful technique for slow readers.[35]

"How do you get fifth-graders to finish a book?" seems to be a common problem. Children must learn when to take only a sample and when the whole book must be read. All teachers emphasize sampling before checking to see if it is really the book one wants, and all teachers point out the value of checking to see if the child did finish the book. "Encourage honesty; and find out, if not, why not." One must be alert for the child who says "there's nothing here for me." A broad selection of titles upon which to draw and variety in book report devices are two ways to help solve this problem. The latter reduces the dislike of books which comes from requiring a number of lengthy written reports. Part of this problem also lies in the fact that the interest of the child is frequently above his reading level. The majority of children, say the teachers, can and do choose their own books wisely, but for those who have not yet acquired this ability, careful and understanding guidance by both teacher and librarian is required. Reading records are a valuable aid in guiding individual book selection and many fifth grade teachers keep their own list for this purpose. Curriculum coordi-

Reading Guidance

nators and reading consultants, in addition, encourage individual reading programs whenever possible and particularly urge the discontinuance of routine group reading.

> Sixth grade. As sixth-grade children become involved in more activities both in and out of school, it becomes more important than ever to encourage recreational reading and to acquaint parents with its special value. Teachers continue to urge reading on one's own level and, simultaneously, the acquisition of the knowledge of how to find books for pleasure and leisure reading. By this time, these children are generally orientated in this type of reading and the use of the library should have become automatic since its facilities are constantly available. Children should be able to discover value in a story, to present short reports, both oral and written, to "learn how to read to get the feeling that the author has had and the feeling he wants us to have," to read for depth and character analysis, and to analyze the whole, not just "the part I liked best." Sixth-graders are introduced also to the use of magazines--to see what is available, to browse and read for self interest and information rather than just to "leaf through."

Although most of the outside reading by sixth-graders is done at home or in the library, teachers do try to find time for quiet reading in the classroom. This is of particular importance in communities where many of the children come from bookless homes, where the adults do not read and, therefore, do not encourage the child to take time to read. The appetite must be whetted by the teacher and librarian. This period, accordingly, along with the teacher's personal interest in the individual's choice of books, continues to stimulate pleasure reading on the part of boys and girls.

Extended reading programs to develop an appreciation of fine books are carried on in a variety of ways. Teachers continue their attempts to follow through on stories and interest leads from the textbooks, constantly stressing the whole book, not just one part of the story. There is evidence of heavy emphasis on science reading among the boys and mysteries among the girls in this group. One teacher found that carefully guided analytical discussions on book characters were quite a successful means to encourage other types of reading.[36] A list of books "strongly recommended to be read before leaving sixth grade," stories which have stood the test of time as well as good modern ones, as developed by one teacher and librarian, is another device used.[37] In another class, suggested book lists include such topics as "Discoverers," "Makers of the Arts," "Fun and Fancy," "Heroes of Progress," "For Pleasure Only." The children report on the books not only through a "retelling in the child's own words but also with a paragraph concerning his special likes or impressions of the way the book was written."[38]

Recordings are used occasionally to explore book possibilities. A record of The Singing Tree by Seredy helped a teacher to stimulate a discussion on reading and use of the library. The conversation following the story time led to an understanding that if there is not a specific use of the library for social studies or science questions, there is always an informal use of it for recreational and leisure time reading. That such an understanding was being developed in this room was most evident. A variety of book report devices indicated considerable reading for pleasure among these children as well as opportunities for creative expression.[39]

Guidance to develop breadth of interest and emphasis on the encouragement of outside reading, therefore, are two of the special problems which are the concern of teachers and librarians working with this grade group.

Reading Guidance

Poetry Appreciation

There is evidence among teachers and librarians in all grades and in all schools of a special interest in poetry. They are concerned that children who respond to it so eagerly, should have the opportunity of becoming acquainted with the best in this field of literature. Too often there has been undue emphasis on rhyme and rhythm and on sentimental doggerel. Adults have been slow to stimulate perception of the magic in imagery. Forced inclusion of poetry which is beyond the experience of the young child or which is didactic in its emphasis has been in evidence. If poetry is to be appreciated or memorized, and the children enjoy doing this if it does not become drudgery or "required," then it should be worthy of the effort.

Teachers draw heavily upon the collections of anthologies in the school libraries to provide poems which fit the variety of moods and the special occasions. Anthologies are welcomed as well for individual browsing purposes.

One sixth-grade teacher used poetry in the read-aloud time in her room. "Children really do enjoy it and it is important to read it aloud. I read many different types, but a teacher must have some feeling for it and not be afraid of it. I try too to encourage my children to put down their thoughts and develop their imaginations."[40] In writing poetry the child should be encouraged to express his thoughts freely and not follow a pattern which an adult may feel is more adequate. It is freshness and spontaneity that are important, not the conformation to rules or an imitation of maturity.

Fifth- and sixth-grade boys and girls seem to enjoy "digging for interpretation." Introduced to anthologies as well as individual collections, one fifth-grade group chose their favorite poems and talked about what they liked and looked for. They learned how to read poems aloud and then memorized them and taped them in order to enjoy listening to each other. They

also compiled an illustrated anthology of their own
favorites. After one sixth-grade teacher had read to
her group "Stopping by Woods on a Snowy Evening,"
they listened to a recording of Robert Frost reading
his poetry. They discussed the meaning of the words
"precis," i.e., what the poem means to me, and "symbolism." They made illustrations of what they thought
the poem symbolized. In a conversation with this
group, it was interesting to note the tendency toward
sadness, almost morbidness, which these children felt
the poem implied. They made up stories which they
thought might have caused this unhappiness. The teacher made no effort to encroach on the individual interpretations with her ideas--an important key to poetry
appreciation--for "one of the subtlest and most valuable
properties of great poetry is that it speaks to the feelings rather than to the intellect."[41] It should be emphasized here that analysis merely as mental gymnastics
is detrimental. An approach which fosters real appreciation and understanding, and which creates a feeling
of the intimate significance of the poem, is the vital
spark in such interpretations.

In another school, when the library's collection
of anthologies was still small, the teachers and librarians prepared a loose leaf notebook, "Poetry Time,"
for each room. It contained poems with which they
felt the children should become acquainted. Although
there are now many fine anthologies in this school library, this introduction of poetry has continued. Each
child creates his own anthology with the teacher furnishing typed copies of special poems. Children from the
third through sixth grades keep a section in their notebooks for their Poetry Sheets. Second-graders and
first-graders after the middle of the year use a little
notebook which they make from colored paper. Children are encouraged to read from their notebooks at
home or orally at school. They become familiar with
many poems and enjoy keeping the collections, often
retaining them from year to year. Occasionally they
read or say their poems in the library, and on special

Reading Guidance   83

occasions they share them over the school's intercommunication system. Some of this school's favorites are "Stopping by Woods on a Snowy Evening" and "The Last Word of a Bluebird" by Robert Frost; "Johnny Appleseed" by Benet; "Beauty" by E Yeh Shure; and "Prayer to a Dark Bird" from the Navaho Night Chant. A few boys in the sixth grade, of their own volition, memorized and shared several passages from Tennyson's Idylls of the King which appealed to their sense of adventure and drama. These children continually borrow anthologies from the school and public libraries. Several children, boys in particular, have purchased anthologies for their home libraries. The teachers and librarian in this school feel that the children are "becoming acquainted with many poems that are their heritage and are enjoying this."[42]

Adventures in poetry are planned with the idea of bringing joy to the reader and not as a discipline. The choice of poetry is most significant. From the nonsense verse to the rollicking ballad, to the sensitive description of scene or mood, from an old favorite to the newest collection on the market, appreciation is dependent upon the teacher and the librarian knowing their children and enjoying poetry with them.

Creative Expression

One of the basic tasks within the broad field of reading for pleasure is that of helping a child to express himself. The library is in a strategic position to foster this creative expression. Broadly speaking, creative expression may take such forms as the graphic type of book report, the program for Book Week, a radio broadcast or a puppet dramatization. But in a more restricted sense it refers to the stories, poems and plays which the children themselves create because they want to.

The best that is available in children's literature presented through those skills of communication—

listening, reading, thinking--frequently leads to a
desire on the part of the participant to express his own
feelings and thoughts. In the early experiences of
kindergarten and primary grades, children delight in
listening for the sheer beauty of the language, the fun
of the story, the excitement of the plot, the rhythm
and music of the poems. As they acquire skill in reading,
they continue to enjoy stories and poems which
retain these qualities and are of high literary standard.
This is followed by the urge to take unto oneself, to
reshape, to enhance and, in turn, to create new stories
or poems, to express and to dramatize one's own ideas
and emotions. This is a very basic part of communication.
It is, furthermore, as exciting and as important
to stimulate children to express their feelings, their
imaginations, their new understandings in the literary
arena as it is in the sciences. One is as vital as the
other for balanced living. Both will stimulate intellectual
curiosity.

    The many fine recordings now available, particularly
with the poet reading his own work, have stimulated
a new interest in oral sharing.

    But the type of books presented, the stories and
poems read with this emphasis in mind must be of the
highest quality. Here the book knowledge of the librarian
and the library collection itself are of great importance.
It is the librarian's responsibility to introduce
to the teacher and the children material which will
foster such creativity of expression. Teachers are
keenly aware of this desire on the part of children and
make broad use of library material. They present opportunities
for spontaneous expression and try to help
children understand and feel what is "good writing."
One fourth grade teacher expressed it this way. "Ability
and ease in creative writing come through because
they have done so much reading of books that they just
want to share their imaginative feelings through their
own writing."[43] Reading both for fun and knowledge
show up in this writing. For example, original Jack

Tales have been "discovered" after a session with Richard Chase's books. Delightful poems have appeared after listening to Vachel Lindsey's, Rachel Field's or Robert Louis Stevenson's poetry. New myths and legends have been created after reading the tales of Odin or Zeus. Space stories have evolved from science books. Even such a prosaic book as The First Book of Bees may stimulate the imagination of a third-grade child. Profusely illustrated, the story about a ride on the back of a bee seems to have the bees buzzing across the pages.[44]

Children also adore nonsense verse, and limericks by the score appear when this kind of poetry is shared. Some rooms have made poetry scrapbooks in which they have collected their own poems, bound them attractively and placed them in the library to share with everyone.

A sixth-grade group listened one day to the teacher's casual reading of ballads. This group was a gifted class, and an idea grew like wildfire. Why not write ballads about their heroes? Jane Addams, Cochise, George Washington, Abraham Lincoln and Babe Ruth were all immortalized in verse at once. One girl in the group was deeply immersed in Moby Dick at the time and her contribution followed that theme.[45]

Creative dramatics is another form of expression which children enjoy intensely. When they are excited about a story such as McCloskey's Homer Price with its humor and adventure, or James Thurber's Many Moons with its "wish for the moon" theme, they delight in sharing it with others verbally. Many of the old fairy tales as well as the modern imaginary stories such as Winnie the Pooh stimulate "playacting." The original plot is retained but the children create their own lines within the vocabulary and environment represented in the story. Legends and folk tales of other lands of the Robin Hood, Roland or William Tell variety, or experiences from the social studies or science areas become dramatic culminations for units of study. There may be a more organized planning of the play with some attention paid to facts, costuming, general sequence and, at least, the pattern of the speaking lines.[46]

Whatever form this expression takes, it fosters an appreciation of the dramatic, of the use of meaningful words and phrases, of the understandings of other people. It points up a need for ability to express orally or in writing one's own thoughts and feelings. This is an aspect of reading guidance in which the elementary school librarian and teacher may make a valuable contribution through the establishment and use of a broad collection of the finest in children's literature.

> Reading Records. To get pupils to use their reading skills, we must rely on feeding children's interests. This is no easy task, and it implies that we teachers must become familiar with the dominant interests of each child not just what he will take without objection, but what he will pursue eagerly. A 'good book' concerned with this interest, written on a level at which he can read without faltering, gives the child pleasure. If he finds pleasure and profit in reading, he will read more.
>
> Let us not spoil the child's fun in free reading by 'questioning him to death' on what is read. Instead, let us find out why the child liked the book, what he considered the most exciting part, what he disliked, and, finally what he would like to read next. If we consistently teach reading skills, and if we are always certain that children are getting pleasure from reading, we may be sure that tomorrow's adults will be better readers than those of today.[47]

Reading Guidance

It is this concern on the part of teachers and librarians to find out the child's own opinion of the books and to guide his future reading that has lead them to adopt the use of many types of reading records and to devise a variety of methods for sharing books.

The majority of teachers in fourth, fifth and sixth grades and some of the librarians in these schools use some form of reading record. They enable the teacher to check on the reading being done; they serve as a guide for child and teacher to prevent lop-sidedness in reading; they stimulate more reading.

In one school the records are kept in a file drawer in the library. A different form is used for each grade; fourth grade, "Reading Record Card"; fifth grade, "Rainbow Reading Design"; sixth grade, "Books I Have Read" booklet. As the children return their books, they indicate them on the proper record. It is their responsibility to record them, but the librarian tries to make sure that a child has completed the book and is not just listing titles.[48]

In another school the librarian has evolved a simple reading record using colored book cards. The first card is orange; the second, pink, and the third, blue. Each card has space for 21 books. When the card is filled, the child brings it back for his next card. Each time he wishes a new card he must show his completed card to the librarian. This gives her an opportunity to see what he has been reading, discuss his books and interests with him and point out ways to extend and deepen his selections. The plan is completely voluntary and may include anyone from second grade on.[49]

On the other hand, many librarians feel that this record keeping is definitely the teacher's responsibility; that such records are a mere mechanism which does nothing to develop true appreciation of books or a sense of the enjoyment in reading, and, furthermore, that it wastes the librarian's time. The informal sharing which the librarian carries on with the classes in the library and with individuals may be of more value in the library program. One danger here lies in over-emphasizing the number of books read rather than the development of breadth of interest, and it is a danger, whether it occurs in the classroom or in the library program.

In discussing reading records, faculty emphasized that "this kind of thing is not good unless the teacher is interested and uses it. She must develop reading for pleasure as well as reading for information. She must make some attempt to help criticize the books read and create an understanding of why this reading is being done."[50] There must also be a reason for the record. One group of fifth grade children gave these reasons for keeping a "Books I Have Read" booklet:

1. It shows how well we read and it shows if the books are all the same type or by the same author.

2. We can recommend a book to somebody else or read it again if it was good.

3. We would know the author, like a special one, and want more of the same kind of story.

4. I know how many I've read!

This particular class goes to the library any time, and they delight in sharing books. They always tell what ones "we haven't finished or didn't like." Their booklets may also be exchanged within the room to see if "it would make another person want to read a book."[51]

One teacher showed a copy of "My Reading

Reading Guidance

Design" to her group, explained the purpose of it and then suggested that each child design his own. Many of the forms were highly original, but all included a place to list the books read and a chart of subject areas in the child's own phraseology.[52] The idea behind such a record had much more significance for the children than the identical printed sheets would have produced.

Six large categories in which all would try to do some reading were chosen by another group. The students discussed what requirements they would have to meet to get credit in the various categories. For example, "a science book you might not read from cover to cover but your report could be a demonstration or an experiment." In fiction, the specific requirements included the usual author, title, comment, climax and some character analysis. Because the children had helped to set up the mechanics for their reports, the teacher felt that the reading response was not only more eager but also more meaningful.[53]

Book reports. The devices for sharing books are manifold. The reports may be written, or oral, or a piece of art work. It may be in a card file or a composition book, either of which may also serve as the reading record. But no matter what the final form, teachers are emphatic in their belief that there should be reports, usually at least one a month; that these reports should list the books read and some evidence of understanding of what the author wished to say; that these reports should not be forced or numerically competitive; that variety in the method of report should be encouraged; that the sharing of reports within the classroom and with other children in the school is an important part of the reading program.

It seems worthwhile to include descriptions of some of the book reports seen in the schools visited. They showed initiative on the part of the children. Informal conversation with these children indicated real enthusiasm for pleasure reading.

All of the written reports include setting, characters, plot summarization and opinion, and emphasis varies with the different types of books and the children who read them. One school system uses the section on book reviews in Mott's Children's Book on How to Use Books and Libraries as a basis for learning how to write good reviews. Occasionally these reports were put into a folder and shared on the reading table.[54] In many other schools the exciting or favorite books are reviewed for the school newspaper.

Card files, both personal and room files, are used almost uniformly in the elementary school as a reading record and report device. The room files are available for all the children to peruse and are a help in finding books they would like to read. In one school each child jots down one sentence about the story and one sentence on his feelings about the book. In another, a longer report is expected. The teacher checks on the titles read and uses these as an aid in guiding reading. In still another situation the child's file is divided by subjects, and he is expected to report books in each area. The large 5 x 8 cards are used for one room's union file, and each child has his own small personal file on which he includes title and date read. Occasionally these file cards are posted in the library and shared with all children in the school.[55]

Many teachers employ charts of one kind or another, such as "Books Are Fun" which holds book pockets for the record of each child, or, "Let's Read More" with two sections, fiction and nonfiction, each one listing a variety of subjects and the suggestion that one from each area should be read. They are intended to indicate variety and not to promote numerical competition.

Oral book reports are shared through a variety of means and are highly popular. One group of fifth-graders had a panel which made notes on the reports according to the following outline:

> Do We Have?
> 1. poise;
> 2. worthwhile facts;
> 3. visual aids;
> 4. distinct speech;
> 5. good English;
> 6. prepared materials;
> 7. time limit.

After the reports the class listened to the panel reactions and then offered further comments on their own. The emphasis here was on positive criticism and audience courtesy, whether the book was new to the group or otherwise.[56]

In another sixth grade the group made tape recordings of their book reports. J--- made a report on Lippincott's The Phantom Deer, and then the class gave a criticism of the review. Said J---, "I made an outline and worked from that." The children agreed that it is better not to memorize the report. One should have his thoughts well in mind and learn to think on his feet. After playing back the tape, they criticized it again and mentioned such points as "she needed to think more about the book. Was it good and why? Was it poorly written or not?" J--- remarked that she was "intrigued because the author wrote clearly and lucidly" and "I felt like I was part of the story." This teacher tried to do at least one such report a day with occasional general discussions and evaluations.[57] The teacher's attitude toward criticism is important in such an effort for it is difficult to develop group criticism that is positive and kind and to avoid inane and trite comments made by children merely for the sake of talking.

The tape recorder is used quite frequently in oral book report sharing. One group played back the book reports which they were planning for Book Week. They practiced listening to their voices and checked to see how they might make the reports more interesting.[58] A recording of the favorite part of a story with varying interpretations was carried on by a sixth-grade group.[59] Another audio-visual aid is the opaque projector. Children show the book jacket or their own illustrations and share the story with the class. A "TV screen" with a regularly scheduled book program was the medium for sharing in one fourth-grade room.

A more formal procedure of oral sharing has been provided by Book Clubs and Story Clubs. Committees planned programs for sharing books through oral reports or skits and dramatizations. One fourth grade delighted in having small groups present five-minute skits of a favorite story and then asking the rest of the class to guess the title.[60] Other clubs carried on correspondence with their favorite authors and shared the letters in class. A sixth-grade organization planned for six oral reports at each monthly meeting, while the rest of the children handed in written ones. A critic made his report at the end of each meeting although anyone else could feel free to comment or to suggest books for fun reading.[61]

"Show and tell" hours were enjoyed by all groups. Children are encouraged to show the book while giving the report and to choose favorite parts to read. Much emphasis is placed upon conciseness as well as on not telling the whole story. A variation of this was done by a fifth grade with a book character party. Each child wore something suggestive of a character in his book and acted out a part of the story. They also shared their books with other rooms through this guessing game.[62]

A rather spontaneous type of oral sharing takes the form of original riddles. Fourth-graders particularly delight in such games. "What was the name of the girl and the book she was in who went to see a wizard?" "Who is the lady who brought a cow on a boat?" "In what book did three little girls climb a big hill?" "I am a little boy caught in a whale's mouth

Who am I?"

Combining art work and book reports seems to be a popular and successful way of stimulating reading. Book character portraits on paper plates made a delightful frieze, "Meeting New Friends," in one room,[63] while another room displayed blue and white silhouettes of favorite book characters. Each picture had a few descriptive sentences about the book pasted below it.[64] Still another grade had made "self portraits" and surrounded them with favorite book jackets to "Explore With Books."[65]

"Illustrating the story," said a fourth grade teacher, "by making a cover for the book can show as well as a written report that they have grasped the story."[66] Such original book jackets appeared in many rooms and in many libraries. Sometimes a blurb was written for the end piece and occasionally a longer review was stapled inside. Pictures to illustrate the story were made for the cover. Figurines for the library, book characters of construction paper or papier-mâché, small dolls dresses to represent a favorite book person and mobiles all appear in this type of sharing. Felt boards or flannel boards were used by several of the younger grades to share a book and by older children in telling stories to younger groups. A special committee from one fifth grade was using the library for help in making a frieze of story book characters composed of the choices of the youngest children in the school through the fifth-grade favorites.[67] "Movies" on broomstick rollers to illustrate exciting episodes in a book were enjoyed, and dioramas or shadow boxes were much in evidence. One lad had made a shadow box for Kintu using small Christmas tree lights. The figurines were made of dowel sticks and a record of African chanting and drumming created atmosphere for the oral report.[68] Stories like The Fabulous Flight, Snow Treasure and Junket all lend themselves to colorful dioramas.

Puppet plays are popular media for book sharing and story telling. Fist puppets which can be made easily by the children are most useful. A spectacular puppet show of some Paul Bunyan tales came from a sixth grade unit on folklore and legends, and an individual's presentation of an episode from Wilderness Journey was equally effective. The old saying, "variety is the spice of life," is certainly applicable to book reports in the elementary schools' reading programs.

A planned program in reading guidance, it is evident, is a basic part of the elementary school curriculum and is the responsibility of both teachers and librarians. To achieve this it is helpful for the librarian to have an understanding of the techniques for teaching reading, and it is equally important for the teacher to have a background in children's literature and reading interests.

Certain desired outcomes which the schools hope to achieve are summarized in one guide as follows:

-development of an appreciation of good literature;
-realization of an inner satisfaction in accomplishment;
-gradual refinement of tastes in reading;
-greater sense of moral and spiritual values;
-enjoyment of many different types of books;
-expansion of interests;
-enriched background of knowledge. [69]

Although these are all intangible results and so somewhat difficult to measure, the progress made by the boys and girls in this direction may be observed by:

-the enthusiasm of pupils' visits to the library and the use of the classroom collection of library books;

- the ability of the children to use available materials;
- the ability to distinguish between desirable and undesirable traits of character portrayal;
- the broadened information in various subjects gained from reading;
- the appreciation of books shown by comments;
- the reports the pupil makes to share reading.[70]

The purpose, then, of the entire reading program, both in the area of curriculum support and of reading for pleasure, is to develop skills, tastes and interests in the field of books. The library serves as the laboratory which provides space and materials for conducting experiments in these areas. Teacher and librarian, therefore, work together to insure that this goal becomes an integral part of the elementary school child's educational program and that reading, whether for information or personal enrichment and pleasure, is an enjoyable experience.

References

1. Mark Van Doren. Liberal Education. New York, Henry Holt, 1943. p. 156.
2. Annis Duff. Longer Flight. New York, Viking Press, 1955. p. 72.
3. Longfellow School, Royal Oak, Michigan.
4. Dewey School, Evanston, Illinois.
5. Euclid School, Jamestown, New York.
6. Parklane School, Fulton County, Georgia.
7. For the result of a study with special emphasis on developmental values and children's books, see Alice Brooks McGuire, Developmental Values in Children's Literature, unpublished doctoral dissertation, Graduate Library School, University of Chicago, 1958.
8. Casis School, Austin, Texas.

9. Cossitt School, LaGrange, Illinois.
10. Casis School, Austin, Texas.
11. Stearman School, Wichita, Kansas.
12. Ibid.
13. Fairmount School, Jamestown, New York.
14. Casis School, Austin, Texas.
15. Meadows School, Fulton County, Georgia.
16. Oakleigh School, Baltimore County, Maryland.
17. Demonstration School, George Peabody College for Teachers, Nashville, Tennessee.
18. Fairmount School, Jamestown, New York.
19. Cossitt School, LaGrange, Illinois.
20. Plandome Road School, Manhasset, New York.
21. Cossitt School, LaGrange, Illinois.
22. Casis School, Austin, Texas.
23. Ibid.
24. Campfield School, Baltimore County, Maryland.
25. Sternberger School, Greensboro, North Carolina.
26. Parkview School, Jackson, Tennessee.
27. Parklane School, Fulton County, Georgia.
28. Fairmount School, Jamestown, New York.
29. Casis School, Austin, Texas.
30. Sternberger School, Greensboro, North Carolina.
31. Washington School, Evanston, Illinois.
32. Casis School, Austin, Texas.
33. Loch Raven School, Baltimore County, Maryland.
34. Stearman School, Wichita, Kansas.
35. Fairmount School, Jamestown, New York.

Reading Guidance 97

36. Casis School, Austin, Texas.
37. Alexander School, Jackson, Tennessee.
38. Ibid.
39. Cossitt School, LaGrange, Illinois.
40. Loch Raven School, Baltimore County, Maryland.
41. Cossitt School, LaGrange, Illinois.
42. Arbutus School, Baltimore County, Maryland.
43. Bush School, Jamestown, New York.
44. Irving Park School, Greensboro, North Carolina.
45. Kiser Junior High School, (special gifted 6th grade group), Greensboro, North Carolina.
46. An excellent chapter in Herrick and Jacobs' Children and the Language Arts. Englewood Cliffs, Prentice Hall, Inc., 1955; "Children's Experiences in Dramatic Interpretations" by Sara Swickard, describes the values of this form of creative expression in some detail.
47. Helen M. Robinson, "Development of Reading Skills," Elementary School Journal, LVIII:274, February, 1958.
48. Brooks School, Greensboro, North Carolina.
49. Casis School, Austin, Texas.
50. Goodman School, LaGrange, Illinois.
51. Munsey Park School, Manhasset, New York.
52. Washington School, Evanston, Illinois.
53. Oakton School, Evanston, Illinois.
54. Greensboro School, Greensboro, North Carolina.
55. Munsey Park School, Manhasset, New York.
56. Lincolnwood School, Evanston, Illinois.
57. Ibid.

58. Irving Park School, Greensboro, North Carolina.
59. Cossitt School, LaGrange, Illinois.
60. Irving Park School, Greensboro, North Carolina.
61. Ibid.
62. Casis School, Austin, Texas.
63. Persell School, Jamestown, New York.
64. Cossitt School, LaGrange, Illinois.
65. Euclid School, Jamestown, New York.
66. Munsey Park School, Manhasset, New York.
67. Sternberger School, Greensboro, North Carolina.
68. Casis School, Austin, Texas.
69. LaGrange School, Illinois.
70. Jackson School, Tennessee.

Chapter IV

"How Do I Find ---?"

Basic to the use of the library in this broad program of curriculum enrichment and reading for pleasure are two areas of instruction for which teachers and librarians are jointly responsible. One is the use of library tools for finding needed information. The other is the effective use of the materials so located.

Library Instruction

Library instruction in the elementary school today is functional. Its overall objective is to stimulate and encourage enthusiastic use of all libraries through a facile handling of their resources. There is no memorization of burdensome and meaningless details beyond the immediate needs of the child.

In all of the schools visited the librarians have an outline of the desirable library skills and habits which they wish to instill before their students go into junior high schools, but in most situations these are flexible outlines. These broad programs, as set forth in the various handbooks or guides, have been based on the needs and requests of teachers and students over a period of years.

During the past ten years there has been a dynamic change in the philosophy behind the instruction of library skills. Evidence indicates that it is now pretty well established that the child is taught a library skill or tool whenever it is necessary. If a child in the first grade has a request for cat stories, he is immediately introduced to CAT as it appears in the card catalog of his school library. He knows that word and it is immaterial whether or not he understands at that point all the rest of the information on the card.

He has made a basic discovery. Here is where he goes to discover what the library contains relative to his immediate interest. Individual instruction is planned to support independent study as rapidly as possible.

No longer do librarians feel that the card catalog must be taught in the fourth grade or the Dewey Decimal classification in the fifth grade. Rather it is assumed that children have already been oriented to the fact that there is a scheme for arranging material and an aid to locating the material. Re-emphasis and enlargement of these understandings has become the key to library instruction. This is carried over in all the competencies or skills which boys and girls need to acquire as they move through the elementary school program. There is always a direct and meaningful relationship with the individual's needs as well as with the classroom requirements.

This does not mean that librarians or teachers have omitted large group instruction from their program. Plans are often made for review of certain tools by the whole class. This is then followed by individual and small group instruction. For example, general orientation in one school is handled through a 20- to 30-minute slide preparation. The series is presented in the classroom and gives general information about the circulation and arrangement of materials, and an introduction to the card catalog. Transparencies are then used for details on the card catalog. Slides show specific location of books, magazines, encyclopedias, dictionaries, etc. This is followed by browsing periods in the library for small groups.[1]

Regardless of the method of presentation, there is a fairly basic pattern which appears in all the schools visited. Two areas, library citizenship and library skills, both of which lead to an increased enjoyment of the library, are stressed. The program begins with the first visits of the kindergarten or first-graders to the library. The librarian introduces them to this new room and makes them feel welcomed. She follows this by simple discussions on the care and handling of books and on library manners. As soon as the teacher indicates readiness, the circulation procedures are introduced. Story hours and browsing periods form a major part of this program.

By the time boys and girls are in the third grade, they have indicated a need to know the location of certain groups of books in the library, such as fairy tales, easy stories or bird books. They learn about some of the parts of a book, i.e., title page, index and table of contents. They begin to have a concept of the use of the alphabet in arrangement of materials in the library, an appreciation which ties in logically with the introduction of the dictionary, the latter generally presented by the teachers. In the fourth grade there is further instruction on the parts of the book and more detailed discussion of the card catalog. Further experiences in alphabetizing, in using various encyclopedias and dictionaries, in discovering groups of materials and types of books available, as well as story hours, browsing, read-aloud and other sharing techniques, are included. Library vocabulary is expanded to include terms such as media, study carrels, filmstrip projector.

The Dewey Decimal system of classification may be explored as a continuation of the more simple generalization of books in interest blocks. Library decimals, incidentally, are often correlated with the study of decimals in an arithmetic class; both Dewey and decimals acquire real meaning. By sixth grade a review of all of this material with details added in each area has been systematically carried out, plus the introduction of simple bibliographic form and new reference books, audio-visual and vertical file materials and the use of magazines for additional and current information. A "Placement Chart for Teaching the Appreciation of Good Books and the Use of the Library" is shown here as an example of one system's overall plan.[2]

Placement Chart for Teaching the Appreciation
of Good Books and the Use of the Library

	Primary Grades (1-3)	Middle Grades (4-5)	Upper Grades (6-7)
Helping Children to Know and Love Books	Informational reading Recreational reading Sharing book experiences	Continuous guidance	Continuous guidance
Introduction to the Library	Library citizenship Circulation procedures Care of library books Library terms and names of lib. tools	Review and practice - Add: Care of recordings Use of magazines Vertical file materials	Review and practice

"How Do I Find ---?"

Placement Chart (continued)

	Primary Grades(1-3)	Middle Grades(4-5)	Upper Grades(6-7)
The Parts of a Book	Physical - front & back covers, spine, body of books Printed parts title page, preface, table of contents	Review and practice - Add: Physical - sections, end papers Printed parts all items on title page, copyright, introduction, illustrations, bibliography, appendix, glossary, index	Review and practice
Classification and Arrangement of Books & Materials	Meaning of "E" Arranged by author	Use of Dewey classificatn. Shelf labels Meaning & location of "F", "B", "R", "E", dictionary Call number	Review and practice 10 main classification numbers Locate special reference books, vertical file, recordings
The Card Catalog	Cards for every book Guide cards, subjects	ABC order Tray labels Cards by author, title, subject as needed How to get call number and find book on shelf	Review and practice - Add: Analyze contents of card; classification no., publisher, date, other information Cross references

Placement Chart (continued)

	Primary Grades(1-3)	Middle Grades(4-5)	Upper Grades(6-7)
Encyclopedias	Persons, places, things and events ABC order Source of pictures "R" location in library	Review and practice Difference between it & dictionary Index vols. Cross references Guides on volumes & pages	Review and practice How to take notes
Dictionaries	Location of "big" dictionary Use of junior dictionaries	ABC order Guide tabs, words Meaning, pronunciation, syllabication spelling	Review and practice Unabridged and abridged synonyms, antonyms Parts of speech
Special Reference Books	Location if interested	As need arises introduce Jr. Book of Authors Goode's School Atlas World Almanac	Review and practice using same Taking notes
Magazines	Location Care in handling Suitable titles	Review and practice Circulation of magazines Source of current information Suitable Titles	Review and practice Scope of more magazines Using and choosing Important Depts. in ea.

Placement Chart (continued)

	Primary Grades(1-3)	Middle Grades(4-5)	Upper Grades(6-7)
Using the Public Library	Encourage the use of the facilities and services of the Public Library by: Visits to the Public Library Public librarian visiting school Bookmobile visit to my school Understanding of financing Summer reading programs, etc.	Stimulation & opportunities at different grade levels	Stimulation and opportunities at different grade levels

    The development of an appreciation of reading, which runs parallel to this program on library tools and skills, is discussed in detail in the chapter on "Reading Guidance." Both phases are basic for balanced use of library services.

    Some teachers prefer to present the parts of the book, the making of a bibliography, the technique of note taking, as an integral part of their language arts study since the English textbooks often include units on the use of library tools. Again, the teacher may introduce a library skill in the classroom while the librarian follows up with specifics; or the teacher may prefer to have the librarian cover the entire area of instruction. Each phase of library instruction must be planned according to the needs of the particular library and its public. The methods of presentation vary, as do the personalities of the teacher or librarian, and the interests of the children are excited in relation to their own curiosities. It is to be remembered that acquisition of skill in use of the library is a gradual and continuous process and that repetition is necessary.

Some of the specific techniques employed by teachers and librarians are included below, but a perusal of manuals suggests many more types of activities which may be employed for this purpose. An interchange of such handbooks among librarians is often of great value in stimulating new approaches.

Although the majority of teachers in third or fourth grades prefer to do their own lessons on the dictionary, it has been found effective to bring the groups into the library at this time to see the different kinds of dictionaries which are available. The third graders particularly enjoy browsing in The Rainbow Dictionary or The Golden Dictionary, and all children are impressed by Webster's New International Dictionary. It is well to provide an opportunity for this group to look up such specific terms as fiction, file, librarian, bookcase, all of which relate directly to the library experience. An early familiarity with the dictionary leads to an automatic and intelligent use of this important tool by the time youngsters are in Junior High School.

An example of teaching the broader uses of the card catalog as they relate to the immediate needs of the classroom was planned by a librarian and a fourth grade teacher. In this grade, where they are busy learning about countries, one special country, such as Norway, is chosen as the basis for the instruction by the librarian. The follow-up with other countries is carried on by the teachers. In introducing the card catalog the librarian reminded her group that they had

"How Do I Find---?" 107

already had some experience with this word "Norway" in the encyclopedia and that it was most important always to have a good mind picture, correctly spelled, of the word. This guidance to all the materials in the library was introduced primarily through the subject card, rather than by the main entry or author card, for elementary children almost invariably begin to inquire for books by subject rather than author and title. The use of the guide letters both on the drawer and inside was carefully explained, and the alphabetical arrangement was shown by large sample catalog cards which the children could handle. The latter were made for specific books in that library on Norway so that there was a minimum of confusion in relating the general examples to the specific. The search for the books on the shelves followed, and the materials were checked out to the room immediately--again a definite learning experience. Both the teacher and the librarian were on the floor to guide the use of the catalog and the search for materials.[3]

The detective approach to the card catalog lesson is a different but quite effective device. This idea, evolved from a book mark from the boys and girls department of the Atlanta Public Library, was used in a fifth grade in this manner. One child decided on a favorite book, such as The Story of Dr. Dolittle, which was "hiding" on the shelves. With the help of the librarian the boys and girls followed the clue (tray labels, guide cards, first word on card); established evidence (class number, author and title); then "X" marked the spot (a search on the shelf).[4]

A review of the card catalog using five or six popular titles, such as Treasure Island, Mary Poppins or Misty of Chincoteague, while the librarian guides the children not only in tracing the books on the shelves but also in finding other interesting information about each book on the cards, serves to pique the curiosity during review and remind children that the catalog is for fun reading as well as informational help. Sets of

Wilson cards--a packet for each child--may be used in a similar fashion to acquaint the children with the appearance of the author, title and subject cards, emphasizing "how much information can you find about the books from looking at the cards?"[5]

    Constant use of the card catalog by individuals and small groups, of course, is the best means of instruction, and the librarian is ever alert to clarify and guide in its use. As the need arises, middle-grade children should learn that the card catalog is a tool in which they may find material on various subjects, may ascertain whether the library has certain titles, and the location of books by favorite or new authors. It is not necessary that they know there should be three or more cards for each book in the library, but it is necessary that they know what cards will be helpful to them in answering questions which their intellectual curiosity constantly stimulates. Children and teachers think in terms of subject and interest first. It is important, therefore, that plenty of subject heading cards, relating materials to curriculum, be developed in the processing center. In this way the card catalog will begin to take on meaning as an educational tool.

    In one fourth grade where the librarian was directly responsible for the encyclopedia lesson, she introduced it, using only one set at a time, by a simple discussion of the arrangement of material: the volume letter, the guide words on top of the page, the heavy print for the subject plus constant emphasis on the alphabetical arrangement. (No mention was made at this time of cross references or index.) Each child was then given a card with a subject written on it--beast, bird or fish--which he was to look up. Several sets of the one encyclopedia were used. The subjects were simple and of current interest. Each child read through his article; thought of one important thing he had learned; put the volume back on the shelf; wrote down his thought in order to share it ultimately with the class.[6]

Another librarian visited a classroom and observed excellent use of the dictionary. This was "very pleasant because it shows you know your alphabet. If you know that, you can use the library reference books, the card catalog and the big dictionary." This provided a point of departure for the introduction of the encyclopedias during the next library period, a step for which the teacher previously had prepared her class. The lesson began with a discussion of subjects in which people are interested--persons, places, events, hobbies and the like. This was followed by the basic information needed to use the encyclopedias in order to learn more about these subjects. Since this group was particularly interested in a hobby show, the librarian capitalized on this. At the end of this lesson the librarian said, "I hope you're not going to be pencil pushers and copy everything the article says! Read it first, and write down what you understand in your own words." Here was a good tie in with the other half of reference work--the use of the information after it has been located.[7]

There is need for constant alertness on the part of the librarian to take advantage of informal opportunities for library instruction. A fifth-grade group studying the middle Atlantic states became very much concerned over the differences in population figures found in encyclopedias and almanacs. This provided the librarian with an opportunity to discuss both census and copyright dates, and to emphasize the need for more than one reference to check accuracy of facts and figures.[8]

Here are a few librarians' ideas for presenting the Dewey Decimal system of classification. It is to be noted, as in all of the preceding discussion, that none of the illustrations given is intended to be taken as the best example or the only method. Rather, they represent starting points for one's own program of instruction.

Children enjoy choosing a large classification, such as the 500's, and breaking it down by tens again and again to see how many subjects can be covered and how easy it is to use decimals, and indeed to determine the kinds of books one might find in a particular collection.

Bulletin boards have been used to teach informally the various classifications of subject interest.[9, 10]

THE "200's"

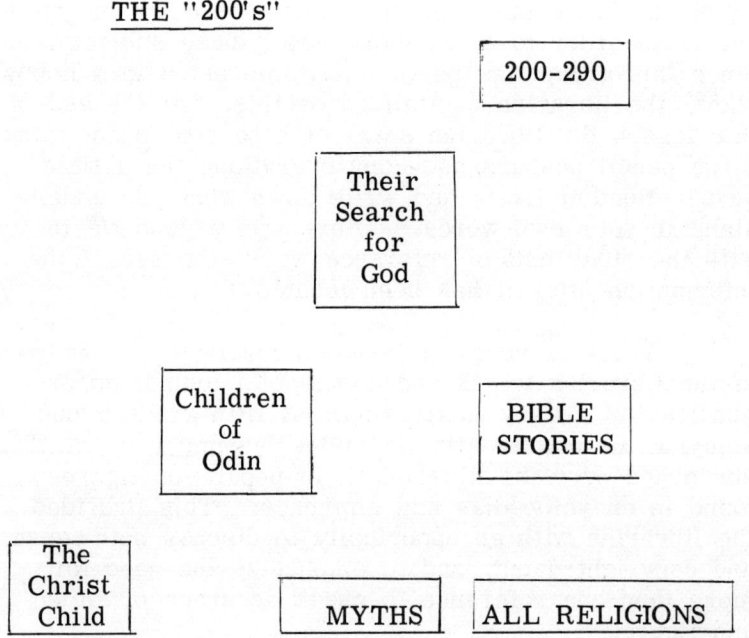

The Dewey Decimal Wheel

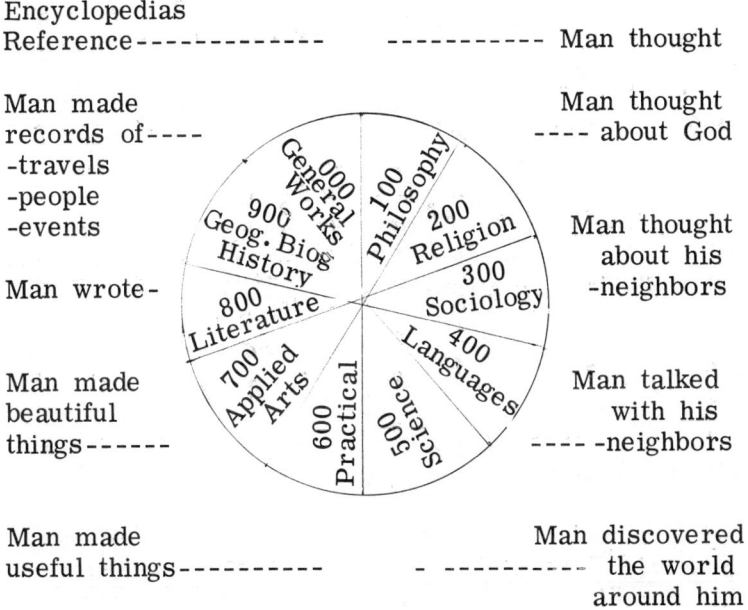

Encyclopedias
Reference ------------- ----------- Man thought

Man made   Man thought
records of----   ---- about God
-travels
-people
-events   Man thought
                                      about his
Man wrote-   -neighbors

Man made   Man talked
beautiful   with his
things------   -----neighbors

Man made   Man discovered
useful things---------- ----------- the world
                                      around him

      A quick and meaningful way of review is available to the librarian when a class begins to study a new state or country. The classification for the continent, country or state is reviewed, the position on the shelf is checked and the numbers on the spine assume a significance in relation to the topic and report.[11]

      One simple technique which may fall under the topic of arrangement, care of books, or library citizenship is used successfully in many schools. The second- and third-grade children are given large strips of cardboard which they mark with their names and decorate as they desire. These slips are used during each library period, after the children have learned

the need for a proper place for each book and each
book in its proper place. As they take a book from
the shelf to read or browse through, the slip of card-
board is placed in that spot marking the home of the
book. If not checked out, the book is returned to its
proper place. In this way the library is kept neat,
and the books are easy to find. The children have
learned a lesson in responsibility and, incidentally,
the busy librarian has one less book to shelve.

Another simple device is a series of mimeographed book marks. These are headed "Encyclopedia," "Improvement in Reading," "Selection of Books,"
Signing for Books Properly," "Card Catalog Helps,"
"Ways of Making Our Library Period More Enjoyable,"
"The Dewey Difficult Child," with information concerning each subject printed below. They are distributed
to the children during the period of library instruction
in which they are emphasized. Duplicates are available in the library.[12]

In one system the librarians use sets of Mott's
Children's Book on How to Use Books and Libraries.
Their own "Outline for Elementary School Library
Program" makes specific reference to Mott and to
the state's handbook for school librarians, as well as
to lists of filmstrips which may be used effectively
in any of the areas of library instruction.[13] In other
schools all references in the English textbooks which
might serve as background helps for the teachers,
along with evaluative questions on each area, are listed in the library lessons section of their handbooks.

Many commercial audio-visual aids are available in the area of library instruction. Among these
are the film The Library--A Place for Discovery;
transparencies, such as Visuals for Library Instruction and Library Series I, II, III, IV; or filmstrips
sets, like Using the Library. Chart racks and felt
boards continue to be basic teaching tools and are
more accessible many times than blackboards. The

librarian must be continually evaluating all of these to be sure they relate to current practices of teaching, have up-to-date references, etc. In most systems, and particularly where there is a good graphics department, it has proved to be of great value for the librarian and teacher to create their own transparencies, slides, informational tapes, etc. so that relevant informative tools can be used in specific situations.

Most librarians check annually for the outcomes of the library instruction program. This is particularly important in the sixth grades where there is need for review before entering the Junior High program. Various procedures have been found effective. One librarian during the spring semester sends to all her sixth-graders a letter in which she wishes them good library usage in the future and lists information about the parts of a book, the arrangement of books in a library, the card catalog, the dictionary, encyclopedias and other reference books, and correct bibliographic form. This serves as a good review technique, but evidence indicates that the letter often reappears in the junior high library.[14]

In another community the librarian, over a period of time and during the regular sixth-grade visits to the library, helps the children put together a booklet. In this they first write the purposes of their school library as they understand them. This is followed by the librarian's list of what is available in the library and the services they may expect. Then comes a section on parts of a book with question and answer sheets for discussion and a short quiz. A page entitled, "You would make a good library assistant if you ...," with a good listing of facets of library citizenship, is followed by a rating sheet and "What Library Assistants Do." Arrangement of fiction and non-fiction books, the use of the card catalog and points to remember about encyclopedias with discussion guides and check-ups complete this aid for future library use.[15]

When planning the library instruction program, it is not necessary to insist, for example, that the card catalog must be taught in the fourth grade or that so many periods will be spent on a certain phase of library instruction, but it is vital to insist that every child in the elementary school should have an opportunity to acquire basic library competencies before proceeding into the more complex educational society of the junior high group. A planned but flexible program is basic to this. Furthermore the concept of transfer--that is, that what the children are learning about their library may be used in other libraries--is a basic educational value.

Reference Work

There is increased need for an understanding of where to find answers in our expanding world of knowledge. However, skill in the use of the tools found in the library is futile unless there is assimilation, interpretation and communication of the information located through these tools. This kind of learning requires skillful guidance on the part of the teacher and the librarian. Much of this guidance is carried on in the classroom as a part of the preplanning which is done before a visit to the library. It follows that the teacher who plans with the librarian and accompanies her class to the library, refreshing her own knowledge of these tools, is far more able to guide pupils upon their return visits to the library, than the teacher who does not know what material is in the library or how to locate it.

In discussing this problem with teachers, several points were constantly emphasized:

1. Teach good study habits.
2. Emphasize a variety of references and not just one article from one encyclopedia.
3. Teach note taking.
4. Teach how each paragraph has one important thing to show.

"How Do I Find---?"

5. Check on note taking through written work as well as through oral reports.
6. Check on note taking through class criticism; i.e., do the children ask questions which show up the inadequacy of a copied report.
7. Help parents to see the importance of guidance in the use of home reference materials.
8. Show how to report in an interesting manner.
9. Learn how to use audio-visual materials for reference work.

"This is the age," said one sixth grade teacher, "when real research begins. The teacher must stimulate the spark of interest in research to avoid boredom and dislike of history and geography. It is her responsibility to show how and where to find the material; to discourage aimless copying; to explain how to write what they can understand, what is interesting and what they can read. If this is done well, the child will continue on his own with enthusiasm. There is a good check here in the attitude of the class. If they are bored by the report, it generally has no more meaning for the student than for the class."[16]

In most schools the reference materials, particularly the most recent sets of the encyclopedias, are kept in the library. But more encyclopedias and other reference materials circulate now on a regular overnight basis. Occasionally, the older sets of encyclopedias may be taken to the classroom for long periods. Another technique is to call in all encyclopedias from every room at the end of the year and redistribute them in the fall so that each room has a different set with which to work. All of these methods have been devised because it is important that children be introduced to a variety of encyclopedias and reference materials. They should learn to go to the library constantly for supplementary materials, for more specific information, for checking on accuracy, for making critical evaluations and comparisons.

Reference work on a fairly formal basis often begins in the second grade. The use of a filmstrip to help in the study of the life of George Washington or the use of transparencies and records in the library to introduce Spanish are examples of audio-visual reference work at an early level. Filmstrips are used in the classroom to teach note-taking by covering up the legend and having the youngsters write down what they think the picture tells them. In a third grade where team teaching was being done, small group work was carried on in the library where books and pictures were examined for relationships to the immediate topic of interest.

A fourth grade teacher reviewed the use of reference materials in her room with the introduction of the new unit on Africa. The topics to be reported were listed on the board as the children discussed their interests. A chart, "What Materials We Will Use," was started. This listed library books to look for by author and title, encyclopedias, filmstrips, supplementary texts, the picture file and so on. A set of encyclopedias had been wheeled into the room, and the teacher explained why one would use Volume A to find Africa, E for Egypt, S for Sahara; the reason for finding Aswan Dam under D; the use of the index for a special topic, etc. It was pointed out that the card catalog would indicate books on food, for example. Furthermore, many of the story books which were being read would also contain information about food and clothing. The index was mentioned as a necessary tool. This summary of library skills preceded the visit to the library for a guided research period.[17]

An interesting review of reference tools which also served as an evaluation of a unit was carried out in a fourth-grade group. The evaluation was guided by the librarian, not the teacher, who remained an

"How Do I Find---?"

observer of the group. For several weeks the class had been studying the sea. During the evaluation session the children explained how they had used the encyclopedia, indexes, card catalog, etc. to find information. The librarian asked how they had taken their notes and what they had found. Children volunteered information about their specific topic of interest. The librarian continually emphasized skills which had been developed and brought in information which supplemented the unit: for example, the Cousteau TV program recently seen, the astronaut who became an aquanaut, etc. It was evident that the librarian had been in the classroom and that the teacher supported the library, an exciting example of reference and research team planning.[18]

Following a different approach, a fifth grade teacher finds a fun reference hour of much value. Before going to the library each child writes down one question. Anything goes--Why do rubber balls bounce? Why does glass break? How do birds sleep? This requires good instruction in reference tools. It encourages the children to try many references. It makes research fun, not drudgery. It also may serve to indicate to the librarian the adequacy of the reference collection.[19]

The problem of how to do significant reference work rather than mere copying was handled by one sixth-grade teacher in this manner. The room was doing a unit in health on the specific topic of bacteria and disease. The teacher presented several books and encyclopedias which contained information on disease. Articles were read aloud. The children helped list the general facts, and the references from which they were read were noted. Following this, teacher and class discussed the different causes of certain diseases, and a list of topics which the children felt were important was set up with this guiding principle: decide what is really worth remembering in one week or three weeks' time. This list became the framework for the library reference periods. It was also pointed out that there were filmstrips in the library which might answer some of their questions, and the technique of note taking was applied to this media as well.[20]

The need to encourage accuracy and critical evaluation may be seen in this simple illustration of a sixth-grade girl's problem. While working on a biography of Nehru, she found discrepancies concerning his birthplace. Her immediate reaction was to go to the librarian, who, in turn, showed her how to indicate in a report that authorities may disagree and that she must then look in several other sources for verification of date.[21] Simple bibliographies result naturally from this type of guided research and are used effectively by the teachers to demonstrate that the source is needed to substantiate statements.

The following outline prepared by one teacher summarizes the processes which should be learned before leaving the elementary program.

Research and Reference Books[22]

I. Preparations for research:
 Step 1: Select the subject.
 Step 2: Locate probable sources of information:
  a. Basic reference books and tools.
   Card catalog.
   Encyclopedias.
   Annuals and yearbooks.
   Indexes.
   Vertical file.
   Special reference books.
   Records, filmstrips, tapes and other instructional materials.
 Step 3; Skim for information on subject.
 Step 4: Take notes.
  a. Do not start copying word for word.
  b. Do not seize first information you read.
  c. Do not take notes on scraps of paper.

"How Do I Find---?"

      Instead--
    d. Skim for information you want.
    e. Try to remember main points you need.
    f. When a source has information you want, write down where you found it (author, title, page, etc.).
    g. Look for topic sentences in each paragraph.
Step 5: Outline the ideas you wish to include.
Step 6: Write paper.
Step 7: Compile a bibliography.

II. Locating information:
 Step 1: Encyclopedias and yearbooks, almanacs:
    a. Give an overview of a subject.
    b. Help you to know a subject.
    c. Yearbooks and almanacs help greatly when you want very recent information.
    d. Learn which encyclopedias have an index.
 Step 2: Card Catalog:
    a. Look for the specific subject (example: BUTTERFLIES).
    b. Look for the general subject (example: INSECTS).
    c. The card catalog will give you the classification number: find books on the shelves.
    d. When books have been found, use the index to find special information.
 Step 3: Use specialized reference books:
    a. Atlases:
     1. General atlases have geographical and political maps, plus maps showing ocean currents, vegetation, climate, population, products, pronouncing index.
     2. Historical atlases have maps showing historical developments.

           b. Dictionaries:
              1. Spelling, pronounciation, definition of words.
              2. Also use biographical and geographic dictionaries.
           c. Quotation and poetry books.
           d. Other specialized reference books.
Step 4:   Vertical file.
Step 5:   Filmstrips, records, science materials, mounted pictures, charts.

References

1. Bowman School, Lexington, Massachusetts.
2. <u>The Elementary Library Handbook: a guide for teaching the appreciation of good books and the use of the school library.</u> Fulton County Elementary School librarian, Fulton County School System, Library Department, Atlanta, Georgia, Rev. 1968.
3. Bush School, Jamestown, New York.
4. Parklane School, Fulton County, Georgia.
5. Munsey Park School, Manhasset, New York.
6. Bush School, Jamestown, New York.
7. Oakton School, Evanston, Illinois.
8. Longfellow School, Royal Oak, Michigan.
9. Hammond School, Fulton County, Georgia.
10. Parklane School, Fulton County, Georgia.
11. Longfellow School, Royal Oak, Michigan.
12. Buffalo Street School, Jamestown, New York.
13. Greensboro, North Carolina.
14. Parkview School, Jackson, Tennessee.
15. Washington School, Evanston, Illinois.
16. Sternberger School, Greensboro, North Carolina.

"How Do I Find---?" 121

17. Parkview School, Jackson, Tennessee.
18. Meadows School, Fulton County, Georgia.
19. Euclid School, Jamestown, New York.
20. Campfield School, Baltimore County, Maryland.
21. Congress Park School, LaGrange, Illinois.
22. Rock Creek School, Montgomery County, Maryland.

Chapter V
Early Elementary Library Experiences

Although the original emphasis in this study was on the fourth, fifth and sixth grade library programs, greater attention must be given now to the services of the library in the kindergarten and primary grades. The most exciting and creative learning experiences in today's schools often take place at this level and the teachers in the primary programs make tremendous use of media centers. Furthermore, experimentation with pre-school learning experiences is a new venture for the school media specialist. The wealth of picture books in the realistic and the imaginative realms and the simple vocabulary used in the short texts make it possible for reading to answer many of the questions with which young children besiege their elders. Librarians provide stories for recreational reading on all levels and encourage youngsters to begin investigation on their own. Non-print media can now be enjoyed early in the primary child's own library experience. The wonderful recordings and filmstrips currently being produced, as well as the easy-to-use equipment, increase the breadth of enjoyment and learning from kindergarten on. Within this age group is laid the real foundation for the delights in reading for pleasure; for the casual acceptance of the library as the place to go because "even in arithmetic, if we find something which we need to know about, we go to the library"; for the basic understandings and skills necessary to use library tools which point one to the right place to find those answers, and beyond that, to the wider horizons of literature, philosophy and science which open up in the teenage years and in adulthood. A closer examination of some of the programs, some of the techniques used by librarians and teachers working with the five- to nine-year old child, will support the above generalizations.

Early Elementary Library Experiences

It is important to include the youngest age group in the regularly scheduled services of the library. Many kindergarten and first grade teachers have expressed the feeling that the pre-reading experiences of their children have been enriched tremendously since the elementary school library included them in its planning. The very first visit which introduces these children into the broader world of books is most significant. Children soon accept the library as a place to enjoy additional story hours and an opportunity to become acquainted with new and exciting picture books. At the same time they acquire certain understandings: how to turn the pages carefully; how to look at pictures; why clean hands are necessary; why soft voices and quiet movements are important.

In schools where kindergartens are a part of the regular school program large collections of picture books and simple information books are on long-term loans from the central library collection. There is a constant effort to enrich and expand these classroom loans. If the picture book collection is adequate, kindergarten teachers are delighted to have their children begin to check out books in the second semester, to share with mother and dad. Undoubtedly, one of the most exciting and happy days in any school librarian's work year is the day when the kindergarten or first-grade children take home their first library books-- the books they have chosen all by themselves. To insure proper care of the book and to encourage sharing at home, it is helpful to send an explanatory letter home prior to the first "take-home" day.

One kindergarten teacher and her librarian have found it effective to work with the mothers' groups to help them enjoy library books with their children. Early in the first semester the librarian meets with the mothers in the library to present book lists of new and standard picture books, to introduce such books as Duff's Bequest of Wings and Larrick's Parents' Guide to Children's Reading and to describe the pleasures in sharing books. The kindergarten teacher follows this with other meetings in the library where the parents share their reading experiences and have an opportunity to browse through library books.[1] In another school in the spring of the year the kindergarteners write their own story books. The teacher writes down the story as the child dictates it, and the latter makes his own illustrations. A special book time is held in the library when the group comes to share its books with the librarian and other boys and girls.[2]

"What do we do when we're learning about things?" So began the librarian in a kindergarten sharing period. "We use our eyes, we smell, we touch," said the children leading nicely into a presentation of books about spring. <u>Find Out About Spring</u>, <u>Hi Mr. Robin</u> were shown and <u>Really Spring</u>, <u>My Five Senses</u>, <u>Sparkle and Spin</u>, <u>Find Out by Touching</u>, <u>First Delights</u> were selected to share in the room.[3] Kindergarten experiences are not just "looking at picture books for fifteen minutes."

Pre-kindergarten experiences motivated by Operation Headstart and federal funds are bringing the school library into the child's life at an ever earlier age. One elementary school pioneered in a reading readiness program for four-year-olds. A series of weekly sessions for pre-schoolers was conducted by the librarian. During the first session she read <u>One Step, Two</u> and a poem about beehives, both emphasizing counting. The youngsters participated confidently. Follow-up activities between sessions for mother and child, such as taking walks and counting things or reading supplementary stories about farms and farm animals, are a part of the program. The emphasis was on books and reading readiness. "We want to point out to parents the many types of activities children can be introduced to through books. We will use the kinds of books that encourage children to talk," said the librarian. "There will be a variety of subjects and geographical areas." Mothers and children were enthusiastic about the experiment as was the principal.[4] More of this type of pre-school sharing needs to be developed and cooperation with children's departments in public libraries and other social agencies is implied.

Listening posts are thoroughly enjoyed by kindergarteners. Not only do the children have a chance to choose the story which they wish to hear, but the librarian can work more easily in some individual reading guidance to those who are not at the moment listening. Careful planning with the teacher to control the size of the group coming to the library, due to the number of listening stations, is necessary.

For many schools where there are no kindergartens this same type of program is conducted in the first grades. The importance of beginning this program with the child's first school experiences cannot be overstressed. Acceptance of books as a natural part of life should have been promoted in preschool programs through the public library as well as through family sharing, but this, unfortunately, is not always possible.

Teacher, librarian and parents must all understand the kinds of books which are being introduced, the ways in which these books may be used, and the responsibilities which parent and child accept when borrowing library books. The library program begins with the immediate experiences of the child in the library, progresses with the taking home of books for family sharing and extends through the very simple story book which the child can read for himself. One such program, described here by the librarian, is now carried on annually in her school.

"Three years ago we planned our first Book Tea in the spring for parents of children who would enter our school the following September. Each family received a booklet entitled 'Read Together-- Grow Together' which included some book lists, pertinent information on books and reading and the following letter:

Dear Parents,

If you had the magical power to bestow two gifts upon your child at birth, what would they be? It has been said that a love of reading and a sense of humor would 'equip a child to deal successfully and serenely with the realalities of life . . .'

A child's love of reading has its roots in the home. It began the first time you read aloud to your child or chanted a nursery rhyme with him. It developed as you continued to share poems and stories with him.

Now that your child is about to enter the first grade, perhaps you are wondering how you can continue to help him with his reading. The school has the responsibility of teaching him to read, but this task will be easier if you continue to share a love of reading with your child. Here are four very good ways to do this:

1. Continue reading good books and poems to your child even after he has learned to read. In this way he can enjoy stories beyond his own ability to read. Make this Read Aloud Time a joyous occasion for the whole family. 'Families that have the habit of reading aloud acquire a common fund of happily shared experience and of memories that last a lifetime . . .'
2. When your child brings his books home, listen to his reading and praise his accomplishment.

3. Buy good books when they can be afforded. Teach your child to care for books. What you esteem, the child will esteem.
4. Encourage your child to use the public library in your community. If you have not joined the public library, be sure to do so now in order that you will be ready to enjoy reading with your child this summer.

In the remainder of this packet you will find aids that may be of value to you in helping to guide your child's reading. Please feel free to consult the school at any time concerning his reading. Indeed it is the school's sincere wish that this next year will mark the beginning of the fulfillment of the many ideals you hold dear for your child.

                    With warm regards
                    Faculty of A---School

"At this meeting we stressed the importance of the family in building a love for reading in the young child. We thought it wise, therefore, to make our library books available to the parents early in the year so that they might share them with their children before the children could read them for themselves.

"After the first graders had had several story hour periods in the library, we sent home a letter to the parents about this plan.

Dear Parents,

Today your child is bringing home a book that he has borrowed from our school library. This is a great event for him, and we know that you will rejoice with him.

Our wish is that both of you, Mother and Dad, enjoy this book with your child. Read and reread it as many times as he asks for it. After supper and before bedtime, as you know, are good times to enjoy a story together. Such pleasant times with good books will help develop in your child a love for reading and give him happy memories to last a lifetime.

Your child may keep this book a week and return it for another on his library day. He may take it to school each day and bring it home at night.

Should you notice that the book needs repair, we would appreciate your marking the page with a book mark and we will mend it.

May we take this opportunity also to invite you to visit your school library which is located in the original school building. We feel that you will be proud of the book collection and facilities that have been made available to your children by the efforts of the Board of Education and your own P.T.A.

> Very sincerely
> Librarian
> First Grade Teacher
> Principal

At the same time, children were becoming acquainted with many books in their classroom and in the library. Very soon they were requesting to take home their favorites.

"As time went on, the children became intimately acquainted with more and more books. If they enjoyed hearing a story in school, that was the book they wished to take home. During this time the teacher charged out the books for the children in the library. But by Christmas most of the children were signing their first name, last initial and room number on their cards.

"After Christmas two-thirds of the children had acquired a rather good sight vocabulary, and we thought it was time to permit them to take home books to read to their parents. We talked this over with the children and then sent a letter to their parents about the role we hoped they would now play in the reading program.

> Dear Parents,
>
> We hope you have enjoyed sharing library books with your children. Indeed, your children have given every indication that you and they have had pleasant times together with books. We sincerely feel that this is one way to build in children a love for reading that will grow as they have contact with books.
>
> Now the time has come for your child to read to you in your Story Hour at home! Perhaps he has already been pointing out to you words he does know in the books he has brought home.
>
> Now he will often be taking home a book that will be easy for him to read parts of to you. There will, of course, be some words he does not know. This is a challenge to him. Give him a chance to work out the words as he has been taught in school. Help him, if necessary.
>
> In doing this we suggest the following cautions:

1. Do not be discouraged if your child has to have help with a word several times. Remember, he is learning.
2. Do not force your child. Reading under pressure or tension has unfortunate results.

Praise your child for his accomplishments and listen with love if he wishes to read the story to you over and over and over.

Yours sincerely

Librarian
First Grade Teacher
Principal

"As a further incentive to learn to read their library books the children were permitted to visit the library in small groups during the week in the afternoon to read to the librarian. A record is kept of the books each child reads, how well he reads it, and what word he has not mastered. At the same time, children are encouraged by their teacher to read their library books to her and to the class. One or more reading periods a week may be devoted in the classroom to oral reading of library books.

"At the present time, mid-second semester, the two best groups of a first grade class are reading fluently and very well:

Brown	Red Light, Green Light
"	Three Little Animals
"	Where Have You Been?
"	Whistle for the Train
Eichenberg	Ape in a Cape
"	Dancing in the Moon
Field	Prayer For a Child
Krum	Four Riders
Lenski	Cowboy Small
"	Farmer Small

Lenski	Papa Small
Minarik	Little Bear
Podendorf	True Book of Pets
Tensen	Come To the Zoo
"	Come To the Farm
Udry	A Tree Is Nice

In addition, the children are encouraged to read from literature, science and social studies books that are supplied in each classroom.

"Teachers and children are enthusiastic about the library reading of the first grade. The teachers say that the children show excellent independence in attacking the new words encountered in their library books. They feel that the children's love for reading is being developed through the challenging content of their library books."[5]

A first grade teacher from another system in discussing her approach to the use of the library indicated that the children begin in the second semester to come regularly to the library to check out books. At this time a letter is sent to the parents. It includes a few pertinent suggestions, such as, decide upon a particular place to keep the books so that they will not be lost, or, try to arrange to hear your child read a little each day. Each child chooses two books each week--one which he can read and another for family sharing. The teacher and the librarian pull out many reading books before the class visit and arrange them on tables according to vocabulary ability. In this way they control the reading and still allow the child to choose from a variety of titles. A large collection of books on units and for pleasure reading are kept in the classroom, but this is not a static collection. Both children and teacher change and add to it constantly. Here, then, the library plays an important role in the school's reading readiness program. The concepts and training begun in kindergarten are reflected most definitely in the first grade's use of the library and parent enthusiasm over the entire library program is high.[6]

Another example of librarian, teacher and parents cooperating on the library reading program for first graders is evidenced in this letter:

> Dear Parents,
>
> We are beginning library reading in our first grade. It is a very important event to your child.
>
> Will you help to keep his interest in library reading by telling him the new words as they occur.
>
> After the book has been read, will you please write a note to that effect and sign your name. The note may be tucked in the pocket of the book. By doing this, we know the child has the book, and the note is used to stimulate reading other books.
>
> We would appreciate it if the children can be helped to assume the responsibility for clean hands before reading. Then many other children can enjoy the books too. Thank you.
>
> Mrs. S----

Some of the notes "tucked in the pocket" indicate parent reactions to these first attempts at reading library books on one's own. It is apparent that the librarian is giving reading guidance:

> Judy enjoyed this book and can do her reading very independently now.
>
> Cathy read her library book four times. Her big third grade sister enjoys helping her with reading when I am busy with something else.

Mark is reading every afternoon now right
after school. He liked this book about one
little turkey who was the luckiest turkey of all.

Skip has read this book several times and
knows all the words so well that he reads
without hesitation.[7]

The books read by the children in all of these
systems are not generally supplementary readers.
Many libraries do not even include this type of book
in their collection. Other librarians make it a point
to include in the easy reading books only those readers
which are not part of the basic or supplementary text
collection in the school.

One must not deprecate the possibilities
for deeper learning experiences at the beginning level
of formal education. An example of a first grade's
introduction to "reference" work amplified this. The
boys and girls in this class developed a sudden and
intense interest in their own state. Although they had
already had a story hour period earlier in the week,
teacher and librarian immediately capitalized on this
new need and planned another library experience.
Discussion in the room brought forth a list of questions
which were printed on an experience chart. This
was taken to the library and, when the class went in
the next day, the librarian talked about the questions
and found the answers for them as she introduced in
a simple fashion an encyclopedia, the World Almanac,
a collection of folk tales and a simple reference book
on Georgia. Not only did the children hear the legend
of the state flower, but they shared the experience of
searching in their classroom, at home and in the library.
Pooling their knowledge and checking it in the
books emphasized dramatically the concept of searching
for answers and using reference tools. They discovered
that the library is more than a place for recreational
experience; that it is also a place to satisfy intellectual
curiosity. Building on this, the librarian and teacher
will advance these youngsters along the way to

independent learning.[8]

Independent reading begins in many schools in the first grade. Rather than using a series of basal readers, the children are given opportunity to visit the library and choose books which they can read and, more important, in which they are interested. This necessitates a real understanding of the children's abilities and interests and a knowledge of book content by both librarian and teacher, as well as great breadth in the collection. The apparent spurt in reading skills would indicate this to be an important technique in the teaching of reading.

The obvious danger lies in the teacher's eagerness to provide the right book for reading instruction. The child may be thwarted in his choice of books or he may associate library books only with the teaching of the skill of reading itself and lose sight of the broader aspects of library service and reading for pleasure. This is particularly true when the child is restricted to books of his grade level. On the other hand, the teacher in cooperation with the librarian can make reading horizons unlimited.

A few school libraries have incorporated ITA or initial teaching alphabet books in their collection, particularly where this method is employed in the regular reading program. Again, the reading ability of some youngsters exposed to this has shown marked improvement,[9] often moving from first-grade level to second- or third-grade level in one school year. The Language Master was used in both classroom and library in one school to encourage children to develop their own vocabulary and create their own stories which they in turn shared with each other. An obvious corollary to this is that the librarian must be aware of whatever methods for teaching reading are employed in that school, the specific needs of the students and must purchase for the collection accordingly.

A science unit on "What is Sound" which asked the children to find out about sounds you cannot hear and all the sounds we hear, stimulated heavy use of library materials. In this room books for the reading table included <u>Book of Satellites,</u> <u>You Will go to the Moon,</u> <u>Moon Trip.</u> Said the principal, "We could do without pre-primers long before we could do without library materials. The knowledge acquired by today's primary age child through TV, etc. demands a breadth of print and non-print media which one or two simple texts simply cannot provide. Indeed first graders need exactly what seventh graders need--only presented in a different manner on their interest level. The library is a supplement to all classroom work."[10]

A visit to one of the first grade classrooms brought forth these comments from the children. "When we first went to the library, she told stories and we looked at picture books like <u>Three Billy Goats Gruff.</u> Now we check out books. We know how to keep them together in a high place and take care of them. We can find out lots of stuff in books."[11]

Among the library skills which seem to be important for first-graders, one finds a knowledge of how to turn pages, how to place books on the shelves so that other people can see the titles, how to check out and return books, how to enjoy story hours and how to browse, and, last but not least, a beginning sense of how to find answers to questions through books. There also should be an understanding of certain library terms, such as circulation desk, book card, librarian, and the development of such attitudes as courtesy, responsibility, sharing.

These aforementioned skills are of definite value by the time a child reaches second grade. This is apparent when one observes the children's activities in their classroom and in the library. One second grade was preparing for a visit to the planetarium. On the blackboard was a map of the solar system to show relative sizes of planets and the length of time it would take to travel to one from the earth. Next to it was a simple terminology list. Weather and the Antarctic expedition were sidelights of this study. The children had borrowed <u>Real Book About Stars</u> and <u>Picture Book of Astronomy</u>, among others from their library. "This type of teaching," added this teacher, "could never be done without a wealth of library materials."[12]

In the second grade next door a "Time Out for Space" question box occupied a prominent place. Any child could write out a question and drop it in the box. These questions came mainly from outside reading, discussions, and radio and TV programs. Volunteers could try to answer them if they wished. At the end of the year these questions and answers will be put into booklet form using primer type so that each child may take his home and read it himself. These children had a specific need to know, which is the beginning of research. They were fortunate in having a teacher and a librarian who made every effort to help them look up answers.[13]

A second grade study on Firemen made full use of the questions on the experience chart. "Do firemen have a back drive from back wheels?" "How do firemen save lives?" "How do firemen hold up the ladder?" Again, the library books were brought to the social studies table in the classroom. Pictures were used to underline the book titles for easy location.[14]

Parallel to the use of library materials in social studies and science are the teachers' efforts to stimulate reading interests and to expand reading abilities through library books. A second grade teacher explored library books with the top reading group. Some children could read on a fourth grade level and were delighted to find new story friends. Most of the library books used in this reading program were of the recreational type. This teacher kept a record of the books the children read by means of a simple book report--author, title and one sentence. She also informed the librarian of the children who needed special reading guidance. This was useful in choosing library books for the room collection as well as in individual guidance in the library.[15]

Another teacher set up a bulletin board, "Free Time For Reading." Below this, on the children's level, she placed an engine and ten cars. Each time a boy or girl read and shared a book, he placed his name on a tiny booklet and dropped it in a car. When he had ten red booklets, one in each car, he began again with another color. This teacher was not interested in encouraging serious competition over the number of books read. The train simply served as one of the numerous game devices which all young children adore, and acted as a stimulant to the child to pick up a library book and read for fun when there was a bit of free time.[16] As any primary teacher can testify, the child's delight at being able to read "lots of books by myself" is very exciting, and the corner in the classroom with a variety of attractive library books is stimulating and beneficial.

An increased use of library materials is found in third grades. One teacher reported that she used the library in all areas, but particularly in social studies. Books, magazines, pictures, filmstrips, in fact, "most of the materials I need, I feel confident I can get from our library."[17] In another system one of the third grade teachers remarked that every science article in the Weekly Reader and all units of work are enriched by referring to the encyclopedia. Any unfamiliar animal or fact in the basic reading book is pursued in library reference aids. This is especially true in science where, in one week, reports were made on the praying mantis, salamander, bald eagle and identification of leaves.[18]

A study of the seasons, and particularly the weather around the Great Lakes, led one teacher to introduce her third graders to Holling's Paddle-to-the-Sea. Intrigued by the story and delighted by the illustrations, the class delved into a study of conservation resources, industry, mining, fishing, lumbering, Indians, geography and animals. They read stories on the history of the area, listened to lumber camp ballads and gathered materials on the Straits of Mackinac bridge. From this came original songs and poems, art murals and a radio script. An interest in narrative development and literary appreciation resulted from discussions of various passages of the story. Such attitudes as tolerance, cooperation and international understanding were by-products of the work.[19] With a good library book as a jumping-off-place and a wealth of library materials to support and supplement the various areas of interest which develop from the children's eagerness to explore byways, an exciting learning experience may take place. This type of teaching necessitates an imaginative teacher and a cooperative librarian, both masters of their crafts. To be of value this must be a spontaneous classroom creativity.

"Matter" was the basis for a science unit in a third grade where the teacher and librarian prepared a relevant science reading list with about eight different books or excerpts suggested. This group was reading in What is Matter, Curious World of Crystals, Beginning Science with Mr. Wizard: Water, Crystal Magic. These children knew how to use the index, glossary, chapter headings, etc. The library instruction was given by the teacher. It related both to the ETV science program and the library materials in the room collection.[20]

In one third grade, an advanced group, the teacher read aloud The Lion, the Witch and the Wardrobe and described the reaction as marvelous. The youngsters did bulletin board illustrations which were

exciting. This teacher had also read aloud most
successfully <u>Call it Courage</u> and <u>Island of the Blue
Dolphins</u>. Today's youngsters grasp mature concepts
even though the reaching vocabulary may be a bit
beyond them. Such sharing always depends on the
level of understanding of the group, and on the teacher's own interest in literature and knowledge of the
general community background and educational level.[21]

    Non-graded programs which cut across the
entire curriculum within the early elementary grades
are to be found in many school systems. An even
richer collection of materials which can flow easily
between classrooms and media center is necessary in
such a situation. The emphasis on ability level rather
than grade level re-enforces flexible planning by all
concerned, with quick, easy accessibility imperative.

    These illustrations of classroom use of library
materials are but one side of the early elementary library experiences. The librarian has a responsibility
beyond that of supplying the materials for curriculum
enrichment. By the time boys and girls finish the
third grade, they should be able to start more detailed
reference work on their own. They should have acquired a knowledge of the simple alphabetical arrangements which are used in the library. They should
understand some of the broad subject areas and the
books which may be found there. They should be
introduced to some of the parts of a book. These are
all essential phases of the program of library instruction.

    As a result of these library experiences and
friendly atmosphere, it is not at all unusual for primary age children to dash into the library with a
treasure found on the way to school (a leaf, a bug or
a snake) and ask the librarian to "please find a book
about this." Or perhaps an experience at home arouses
a special interest in the library. One first-grade child
whose next door neighbor was an ornithologist went
through the whole bird book collection in his school li-

brary, looking for books with pictures of the birds, nests and eggs about which he had heard. One would not rate M---as a gifted child, but his knowledge in this area was amazing and his interest sincere. He took it for granted, furthermore, that the library would have what he wanted. How tragic it might have been if he had been limited to those books which were on a first grade reading level, or to the handful of general materials in a classroom library.[22]

One of the basic needs, therefore, in every elementary school is a centralized library with a collection of informational books and materials large enough in reading levels to answer the need of the questing mind of the primary child.

Literary appreciation also begins with the primary child's visits to the library. The picture books, folklore and poetry available for the elementary child is infinitely rich. Librarians have a responsibility to select the best from an overwhelming number of new titles each year and to present this material in such a manner that a sincere appreciation for literature is fostered.

Story hour groups, with or without picture books, but using the technique of the true storyteller, is one of the effective ways of making this heritage an integral part of the child's background. Artificial devices such as puppets or flannel boards or a good recording occasionally may vary the presentation, but the key here is the story itself told by word of mouth. To present during story time a picture book composed of a series of fire engines or trucks because "children like engines" or "it ties in with the unit," rather than to share the warmth and excitement of Mike Mulligan and His Steam Shovel, for example, or the humor of The Duchess Bakes a Cake, is like forcing an adult to read a pulp magazine when he would much prefer the Atlantic Monthly. It is a serious form of brainwashing and a step in the direction towards mediocrity of the masses. Thus, a story which is vital, rich in

Early Elementary Library Experiences

word descriptions yet simple, full of the wisdom a young child can comprehend and which is related easily in an informal face to face situation is one of the finest experiences the children and librarian may enjoy.

This is, furthermore, the age for the repetitive story and offers an opportunity for the librarian to introduce the old folk tales of <u>Three Billy Goats Gruff</u>, <u>The Old Woman and her Pig</u> or <u>Lambikin, Lambikin</u>. The traditional fairy tales of <u>Boots and his Brothers</u>, <u>Cinderella</u>, <u>Jack and the Beanstalk</u> and many others continue to increase the child's cultural heritage as he matures and comprehends the more complicated plots. With the finest of the old enhanced by the best of the modern, literary judgment is developed for selection and appreciation.

Children rejoice in the best that is presented and very soon are able to ask by title for special books and stories. Most of the library manuals examined include lists of excellent stories for telling as well as lists of books with which children should have the opportunity of becoming acquainted sometime during their first three grades in school. Illustrators such as Beatrix Potter, Wanda Gag and the Caldecott award winners are emphasized. Guidance in intelligent browsing is discussed. During picture book hours or sharing groups, the librarian may point out the author's name to see if he is a new or a familiar friend; may indicate the name of the illustrator and suggest that his pictures have been in other books; may invite the children to show and tell about the book which they have been enjoying that week. When new groups of books are to be put into circulation, the librarian may point out easy and good stories for reading, share some of the outstanding illustrations or capitalize on the beautiful new editions of old favorites.

One second grade group thoroughly enjoyed listening to taped stories at the listening table. <u>Bre'er Rabbit and Tar Baby</u> was a favorite. The stories were discussed with the librarian afterward. One found it quite enlightening to watch the facial expressions of the listener and to hear the exclamations even though the observer could not actually hear the story.[23] The use of filmstrip and record combinations, such as those from Weston Woods, are popular and a real addition in fostering literature appreciation.

It is vital to include full library services to all children within the school community, beginning with the youngest group. A curriculum coordinator expressed it this way. "One must start the full library program with the kindergarten; then sharing books will continue through the school. Children in the first three grades will enjoy reading to the kindergarteners. In the first grade, science units and social studies work must be supplemented right from the beginning with pre-primers and picture books. In the second grade children find supplementary reading books to help in social studies, science and arithmetic story problems. In the third grade they begin building dictionary understandings. Parallel to this, the children will be led to story collections and interpretive illustrations. The library is the key to the curriculum. It fills in around the skeleton."[24]

Services related to all the aspects of curriculum materials plus the interpretation and presentation of the best in reading produce satisfying library experiences for the early elementary children. As one primary child said, "I wish all schools everywhere could have a library just like ours."[25]

References

1. Fairmount School, Jamestown, New York.
2. Bush School, Jamestown, New York.
3. Chisholm Trail School, Wichita, Kansas.
4. Stearman School, Wichita, Kansas.

Early Elementary Library Experiences   143

5. Arbutus School, Baltimore County, Maryland.
6. Washington School, District No. 65, Evanston, Illinois.
7. Orrington School, District No. 65, Evanston, Illinois.
8. Mt. Olive School, Fulton County, Georgia.
9. Campus School, Western Michigan University, Kalamazoo, Michigan.
10. Mt. Olive School, Fulton County, Georgia.
11. Meadows School, Fulton County, Georgia.
12. Dawes School, District No. 65, Evanston, Illinois.
13. Ibid.
14. Buckner School, Wichita, Kansas.
15. Dawes School, District No. 65, Evanston, Illinois.
16. Ibid.
17. Longfellow School, Royal Oak, Michigan.
18. Irving Park School, Greensboro, North Carolina.
19. Longfellow School, Royal Oak, Michigan.
20. Oak Knoll School, Fulton County, Georgia.
21. Glen Haven School, Montgomery County, Maryland.
22. Campus School, Western Michigan University, Kalamazoo, Michigan.
23. Parkside School, Montgomery County, Maryland.
24. Jeanne Brouillette, Curriculum Coordinator, District No. 65, Evanston, Illinois.
25. Bear Creek School, Baltimore County, Maryland.

Chapter VI
The Teacher and The School Library

Significant Areas for Teacher Librarian Cooperation

In order to make the library a tool of curriculum enrichment and to facilitate the services of the library to all the children of the school, there are certain phases of cooperative planning which should be stressed. Teachers and librarians may be expected to work closely together in specific areas of the library program, such as selecting the book collection or programs for classroom visits to the library, as well as in curriculum development, faculty committees, in-service training, bibliographies for units of study and presentation of new materials.

Teachers have an important role to play in the maintenance of the caliber and content of the library's media collection. The librarian is constantly aware of the new titles which become available and tries to note the gaps in the collection which appear as various curriculum questions arise. But the teacher with her specific classroom interests and knowledge and her actual use of these materials is in a strategic position to suggest definite areas of need and titles of books. She may make specific suggestions from bibliographies in the textbooks, from books which she has examined at educational exhibits, or she may point out subjects and interests which are in need of broader coverage. The same process applies to non-print materials.

Librarians encouraged participation in book selection at all of the schools visited and in a variety of ways. They may make available catalogs, lists and order cards. They may accept suggestions at faculty meetings. In one system exhibits of new books are sent to each building with an annotated list and a letter urging the teachers to examine and check for future reference. A copy of their special wants is given to the librarian for ordering. This has proved a profitable technique to arouse interest in ordering and to bridge the gap between the old classroom library idea and the new broader centralized library concept. Consultation with the curriculum coordinator as well as with the reading specialist is a regular part of the library program in many schools.

Careful planning by teacher and pupils before library visits has been mentioned at various points throughout this study. But the techniques which are used by the teacher and librarian to guide this pupil planning and to make the library period itself more meaningful to the children need further amplification.

Generally, teachers plan to come in ahead of the class period to talk over special class needs. They come in their free time or before or after school to browse. It is particularly important for them to check on materials before a large or new unit of study is begun. It gives the librarian background, but it is even more important for the teacher to be sure that there is sufficient material available on the subject to avoid a frustrating library experience for the class. Likewise, the teacher is careful to tell her pupils if she has borrowed from the library all this material for classroom use before the group descends upon the librarian. Contrast this planning with the teacher who with no warning sends to the librarian a checklist of subjects on which the children in her room will now be doing committee or individual work.

Team teaching of non-graded programs re-emphasizes the need for closer planning. Team teachers find that they make more use of the library. There is more freedom for their own special study period. They are more likely to be involved in small group work in the library for special study and discussion. All units must be planned carefully to determine what activities are going to be developed; what supplementary background is needed; what directions the small groups might take; what type of library instruction will be needed. One librarian commented that at last she could really get into the classroom and work with the youngsters. The librarian can really do some of the teaching, introducing the materials she knows in depth. Likewise in the non-graded program, teacher and librarian must be fully aware of the ranges of comprehension, the breadths of interest so that significant materials may be made available as needed. In both instances the flow of materials and children between classroom and library center is continuous and in both directions.

Teacher participation in the library during the class visit is very important. One superintendent emphasized this in a bulletin to teachers.

> Because a classroom teacher must be aware of the impact of all of the other personalities and programs on children, it is imperative that each classroom teacher keep as close a check as possible on what teaching goes on in each special teacher's class . . . . Specialists are helping classroom teachers because they have specialized skills, and because no one person could learn all of these skills to the high degree of proficiency we would like to offer our children . . .

> When the problem is viewed in this light, mandatory attendance by the classroom teacher at every special class is not the significant aspect of the situation. She should feel compelled to attend many or most of the special classes in order to better understand what is being taught, in order to better understand her children seen in a different setting, and to help in the transfer of good habits from one area of living to another. By the same

token classroom teachers should occasionally, as time permits, attend other group meetings to which she is invited in any one of a wide variety of fields in order that she may better understand the philosophy underlying the activities in those fields. . . . Each one of these professional people is important in the school lives of children. It is the classroom teacher, however, who must be the contact figure, the coordinating agent, to bring unity out of the many types of experience offered to her children.[1]

In another system the stated responsibility of the classroom teacher is "to work with the librarian during the library period to establish good class habits and to see that each child finds and uses materials suited to his interests and abilities; to take advantage of the library period to observe and guide the reading of individual students."[2] In no way does this compel the teacher to sit in the library during the entire class time but, as one teacher expressed it, "Most conscientious teachers realize they can contribute and learn from the library period."[3] Participation in library instruction not only refreshes the teacher's knowledge of library tools, but also helps her give specific guidance to her pupils. Conversely the librarian must go into the classroom. She must be aware of how materials are used and the variations in learning experiences.

Many schools participate in programs of student teaching and this provides a fine opportunity for demonstration of the use of the elementary school library. Classroom teachers in such situations feel that the student teacher should "come right in with the class and the teacher and stay to work with the pupils in order to develop a better understanding of how the library program works." They also believe that the student teacher should be brought into the library immediately for orientation, that he should be especially invited to participate in the library instruction classes and that he should receive guidance from both teacher and librarian in the actual selection and use of library materials. This is an area which needs emphasis in all student teaching programs.

The attitude of the teacher toward the library has a direct bearing on the children's attitude and use of library facilities. The teacher who brings her class to the door and leaves them surely cannot expect to have enthusiasm for reading or reference work, or for the exploration of new and exciting interests in her room. These are apparent in the classroom where the teacher herself enjoys the story hours, shares in book discussions, is obviously keen on reading for information and, above all, passes on this enthusiasm to her boys and girls. The librarian in turn has a responsibility in the school's program which may provide valuable assistance to the teachers. Basic to this is the acceptance of the librarian by the administrator as a regular member of the elementary school teaching faculty. There are many ways in which the librarian may supplement curriculum planning. She may work directly with the curriculum coordinator, or, as in many elementary schools, serve on the overall curriculum committee or on a specific subject area planning committee. In this way she may contribute information on the availability of materials relating to curriculum problems, help plan bibliographies for courses of study, demonstrate materials, participate on panels, aid in scheduling to avoid simultaneous study of units in the same grades or, if this is impossible to change, suggest how best to share materials. Wise duplication of materials within the library also helps. Special bibliographies covering a variety of grade levels were prepared by one librarian on such subjects as: <u>Books to Grow on for the Kindergarten Child</u>, <u>Famous Americans for Young Americans</u>, <u>The West</u>, <u>Regional Stories of the United States</u>, <u>Pooks for Slow Readers</u>.4

There is danger in making detailed book lists for units. In her eagerness to help, the librarian may be guilty of spoonfeeding the teachers. If that happens, little real reference work is carried on and it often results in stereotyped unit planning. It is possible for the busy teacher to rationalize that it is no longer necessary for her to come to the library. A mail-order catalog technique is developed, and the growth and understanding which is a natural result of personal consultation with the librarian is too often lost. To be sure, the librarian is ready at any time to answer a special need or immediate request, but the long-range planning and choosing of materials for the constructive use of library materials is a matter of joint responsibility.

Most elementary school librarians have provided a professional shelf for faculty, either in the library or in the staff room, which includes current professional magazines, books relating to educational philosophy and curriculum planning, bibliographies of general interest to all faculty and marked articles of pertinent value. In addition, materials are borrowed from the centralized professional library.

Several librarians display new materials during faculty meetings and discuss library problems which need school wide consideration. Joint teacher-librarian faculty committees are designed to coordinate and encourage broader understanding of the library's resources and potentials and to help in policy making. The presence of librarians at grade level and department meetings also has a direct result on the teacher's use of the library.

Inservice training and orientation programs are other helpful ways to develop library competence on the part of the faculty. New teachers have private conferences with the librarian to learn the special features of their particular school library. In one school part of the fall inservice training program for new teachers is given over to library orientation. In another, a looseleaf notebook, "Your Library Has For You," is given to all teachers. This indicates check-out procedures, student aid policies, professional materials available, a floor plan of the library, services available, student policies, suggestions for teacher librarian planning.[5] Sessions to orient all teachers to audio-visual equipment and materials and their use in the teaching program are basic. Administrators feel that this is an important part of library service.

This is a two-fold program in cooperation. Although the librarian rightfully expects participation from the teachers, she must also develop her skills in human relationships. She must respect the standard of her fellow teachers as well as retain her own professional values. She may make reports on the progress made in the use of the library, but she must also exert an effort to implement, to broaden and to interpret the services which she hopes her public will use. In turn, the teacher will express her interest in the overall development of the library program and continue to expand her use of the library facilities.

Teachers' Background in Children's Literature

Librarians in elementary schools feel an urgent need for increased training of teachers in children's literature and in use of the library. In every school system visited one or more of the intermediate grade teachers emphasized the value of such courses. The librarian may make materials available in quantity, but the teacher is responsible for building an appreciation for good books through a continuous reading program in the classroom.

Said one fifth grade teacher, "I wouldn't take anything for my course in children's literature. Teachers must have definite background in the use of library services. Too often lip service only is given to this and there is not enough practical experience in an elementary library with a program and materials." "We take too much for granted with our university students," remarked another teacher.[6]

"All teachers in our system must have a children's literature course," said one librarian. "But it is evident that they also should have an introduction to the use of library materials."[7] Teachers who have had a good course in children's literature do much individual guidance in reading and work with parents to encourage summer reading. They cooperate closely with the librarian both in curriculum planning and in reading for pleasure projects.

"Teachers just must be dependent on the librarian for keeping up with the new and best materials," said a sixth grade teacher, "but they should take a course in children's literature for a refresher. You will know more about the books on which the children are reporting and can pick up more quickly from their reports the new stories and books."[8] That there is a personal need for this background among the young teachers was expressed by a teacher in a county school who indicated that a teacher surely could use a specific course in children's literature and that she needs some guidance in the use and services of the elementary school library too. One who has had good reading background as a child has a definite advantage over teachers who have had a weak literature program.[9]

In one school the principal was taking a course in children's literature and was finding it of value in his work with teachers and students as well as in his understanding of the librarian's program.[10] "Children," said another principal, "have the utmost faith in the library, but teachers must be led to learn how to use it and implement interests."[11,12] It is evident that this is an area which needs strengthening. The teachers themselves are keenly aware of its importance.

References

1. Superintendent's Bulletin to Teachers, Evanston, Illinois. (Mimeographed).

2. <u>The Elementary School Library</u>. Bulletin, Office of the Supervisor of School Libraries, Baltimore County Schools, Maryland.
3. College Hill School, Greensboro, North Carolina.
4. Bush School, Jamestown, New York.
5. Meadows School, Fulton County, Georgia.
6. Casis School, Austin, Texas.
7. Parkview School, Jackson, Tennessee.
8. Cossitt School, LaGrange, Illinois.
9. Oakleigh School, Baltimore County, Maryland.
10. Loch Raven School, Baltimore County, Maryland.
11. Alpharetta School, Fulton County, Georgia.
12. See also Chapter on the "Role of the School Administrator" for further administrative comments on this need in teacher training.

Chapter VII

The Role of the School Administrator

> With the exception of the staff itself, the library continues to be the greatest single resource for the realization of the purposes of the school.[1]

It has been emphasized repeatedly that the teacher and librarian are working together constantly, supplementing each other's knowledge of books and children in order to insure a rich use of the library's services. But what about the curriculum coordinator, the principal, the superintendent--all who are concerned with the unification of program, the development of sound educational principles, the direction of the teaching goals? Do they have responsibilities in this library picture? What is their philosophy concerning the elementary school library? How do they feel about teacher-librarian relationships? Are there specific suggestions they would make to further implement the program?

The administrators in the schools contacted in this study are key people in the future development of the elementary school library program, both within their own systems and nationally. They are keenly aware of the fact that there are far too many schools with little or no elementary school library service and, that, as a result, far too many children are being deprived of the opportunity to broaden their understanding of peoples and society and to expand their intellectual capacities. It is interesting to note that the basic concern has not changed in the last decade even though the phraseology may be more modern!

Their comments have been divided rather arbitrarily into three categories: (1) what the administrator thinks constitutes a good elementary school library; (2) what the administrator's responsibilities are toward implementing this program within his own school; (3) what the administrator thinks might be helpful in beginning or expanding the elementary school library in his own or in other communities.

Administrative Philosophy

Considering first what these administrators believe is important about an elementary school library program, it becomes apparent that these quotations include their general philosophy as well as their observations on the specific services which they feel should be offered.

"The elementary school library can introduce one to the repository of independent education through good guidance. The library is an enrichment area that must be used and developed. The school should make good use of the specialties of the librarian. She is the explorer of the reading interests of the child. The library is supplementary to, not subordinate to, the central functions of the classroom. It helps forward the coordination of the basic skills. The library does one of the best jobs in the reading program. The library period should be constructive to justify the children leaving their classroom. In other words, it must meet the teacher's needs too. It enables her to escape being tied only to the textbook. In this enrichment area the specialist is in charge and the classroom teacher may serve as her assistant. The elastic program of the centralized collection is valuable."[2]

"The greatest thrill comes from seeing this complete integration--this spark between teacher, children and librarian. Atmosphere is basic in today's media center. Furthermore, the use of many media helps overcome blocks and emotional tensions. Youngsters just come into the library to relax--to get away from the classroom. The library is a privilege and there is no real discipline problem because they know their way around from kindergarten on. There is absolute freedom to come and go between the library and the classroom. We use, we live with, we believe in the library."[3]

"If you do not have a library you miss the dynamics of the whole thing. It is the key to all the learning in the elementary school. Textbooks are a confined sort of learning. Materials and an enthusiastic staff make all the learning really come alive. It is a continual situation. Classroom and library reinforce each other. The library program is important to the whole school system's program. When a child comes in with a worm and we wonder if it has eyes, we just know Miss _____ has a book that will tell us. We go down then because we can catch and reinforce the child's excitement for learning. We know the library has what we will need."[4]

"The library is the key foundation stone to the social studies and science programs and a key position in the reading program," said one principal. "It is absolutely paramount to a good teaching program today. My teachers would object strenuously if the library were now withdrawn. Having the library started as soon as our school program developed helped stimulate use."[5]

Amplifying this thought still further, another principal expressed his belief that "the library must function as a service center for the instructional program of the school. This, of course, would mean that it would not only provide books, movies, filmstrips, vertical collections, maps, globes, professional materials, but would provide instruction in the use of libraries and research type activities. This is a big order and proper staffing is essential. Such a service would have to be housed in adequate facilities-with ample room for children, books, materials and work space for the librarian and her assistants. I see the librarian not as someone who is burdened down with chores of book handling, mending, etc., but one who has the time and opportunity to interest children in good materials, wide reading, skills in research."[6]

Again administrators point out the value of the library to the individual child.

"The library fits in so well with individual differences of children. We cannot begin to take care of the gifted children without it. The librarian assists the teachers in research work in all areas. Children are intrigued by and proud of our new library. The increased reading shows it. The library should be open the entire school day so children may learn to appreciate it and use it properly. The teachers can capitalize on a child's interest the minute it arises. It is important today in relation to the renewed science interest."[7]

"For a good school library there should be adequate space and suitable personnel. There should be central processing so that the librarian may be available for children's needs and services. There should be some form of summer library service for a twelve month enrichment program. Reference materials should be centralized but mobile. A reading center in the classroom is desirable, but a classroom library will not suffice for a central library. Moreover, the library is the one best instrument for serving all children--handicapped and gifted."[8]

The need for children to have special instruction in the use of the library and its basic value in the instructional program of the school is emphasized repeatedly.

"No student or group of students should come or be sent to the library without a definite purpose in mind. This might be to be taught the library skills, to check out books, to do research, to enjoy stories read or told by the librarian or to read for pleasure.

"The most convenient location for the Teachers' Professional Shelf is in the library where the teacher may snatch a few moments to browse or read while her students are being taught by the librarian or are carrying on activities which do not require her immediate help."[9]

"How can we dare to limit the amount of materials available to children. It is sheer shortsightedness. It is impossible to get it all from texts or TV!"[10]

"We want children to read for recreation but we feel that the library's greatest value stems from its use for research. Additional books on any subject add facts, interest and enthusiasm to the instructional program."[11]

"The library is the hub of school activity. Academic and fundamental work are based absolutely on it. The library helps children to develop inquiring minds about everything. It is a place to go to solve the problems themselves. Research periods are important. Children learn at the very lowest level with proper procedures. The faculty send children to the library with a purpose. Actual space in the building is vital, and a trained librarian with teacher background is essential. The library is in essence a place of quiet and study. The care of materials reveals good citizenship. Order in a relaxed atmosphere is important."[12]

"The modern school is dependent on the library for effective teaching. The curriculum is dependent on these extra sources. It improves reading in school. It is a source of enrichment for accelerated children."[13]

Most of the statements by curriculum coordinators are found in appropriate places within other chapters. But, the philosophy upon which the coordinator acts as a member of the administrative staff is pertinent to the development of the elementary library program. These next comments, therefore, are particularly relevant to this chapter.

"The librarian keeps me informed about all new materials. She helps teachers who lack a strong academic background. The library is the center for distribution of many materials. To use it properly one must be thoroughly acquainted with all that is available. The children need the cultural enrichment which is imparted through this vital part of the school--the library."[14]

"The elementary school library is important in the lower grade reading groups where they need books for information, for comparison and for fun. The library provides a wealth of good literature for all levels of reading. It helps in encouraging research skills in the elementary grades. It helps with interest reading groups and with groups which should be reading library books rather than basic readers. Frequently when the basic reader is finished a child can be motivated to broaden his reading interests by selecting varied types of library books for review and/or reporting to the class. The library exists for teachers and students, and the librarian contributes greatly to curriculum enjoyment, depth and strength."[15]

"As a Curriculum Coordinator, I try to help each new teacher to make the best possible use of the materials and services in our school libraries. During my own years of teaching I discovered the value of using children's reference books as an adequate and readily available source of background information for teachers. Often materials of this type are sufficient to meet immediate needs.

"In the field of reading the child receives his instruction in the basic skills in the classroom. Practice in the use of these skills is provided for all children through the close cooperation of librarian and classroom teacher."[16]

Role of the School Administrator

In connection with these services which they expect from the library, the administrators have some very pertinent things to say about the librarian herself.

"The librarian must have a good teaching background and an understanding of the needs of the classroom. She must adapt herself to the system's techniques. She must have a knowledge and understanding of child growth and development. She should be able to work well with colleagues and parents, have a pleasant voice, be attractive in appearance and possess enthusiasm."[17]

"The needs of the elementary school librarian's professional education is different from other librarians! She must include teaching background and an understanding of the curriculum. She provides for pupils' and teachers' skills and services that a classroom teacher cannot be expected to possess or render. She must make available the maximum resources with the minimum of effort and least loss of time."[18]

This idea was reiterated continuously. It is obviously a point about which administrators feel keenly and to which librarians and directors of library education programs should give serious consideration. Additional statements point out other specifics. One principal said, "When the librarian seems to understand classroom problems, it makes for better teacher understanding and interplay. She must be a curriculum conscious librarian."[19] While other colleagues included such amplification as: "The librarian cooperates wholeheartedly with the teachers. They feel she is an authority and knows the individual children."[20] "The librarian's personality is important in school relationships. She must promote her services with teachers who have less background in library use."[21]

"The librarian keeps the principal informed concerning phases of the library program which are vital. She is skillful in helping teachers to make good use of the library; helpful in leading the child beyond the classroom. She must work closely with the building curriculum coordinator. The personality of all librarians is vital in any program, and the enthusiasm of the college librarian in a teacher training institution may well be most important in influencing the future use of the school library on the part of teachers."[22]

"We hold to the theory that the librarian should be a curriculum materials expert and that the bulk of her time should be spent in helping teachers and children know what is available and how to get the best use from it."[23] In other words, as one administrator expressed it, "This is a two way street. As a professional person the librarian must prove herself through her services to teachers and children. The success of the library program is in her hands."[24]

Administrative Responsibility

What can administrators do to implement the program of the elementary school library within their own schools? Mr. B. L. Smith, Superintendent of Schools, Greensboro, North Carolina, writing in The School Executive, expressed his belief in this statement.

> The School Library is really only as good as its superintendent desires it to be. He is the key person, in other words, in developing libraries and library services. For budget making, facility planning, personnel employment and service utilization are all responsibilities in his bailiwick. . . .
>
> Fortunate indeed is the school system whose superintendent knows how essential library service is and gives leadership in making it available. It is his duty to convince his board of education and his patrons that:

Role of the School Administrator 161

> Every school should have a library.
> Every library should have the services of a trained librarian.
> Every school system should have a cataloging department and materials center.
> Every teacher should have a knowledge of children's literature and skill in the utilization of books and other library materials.
>
> The necessary taxes should be raised to provide space, materials, and staff to operate the library. . . .
>
> We do not ask that the superintendent of schools be an expert in library skills and techniques. But he is expected to be aware of educational advances and to inform himself of the part he may play in the improvement of public education . . . .He should acquaint himself with the literature in the field of library service. . . .
>
> Through his policy recommendations, budget preparation and instructional guidance, the superintendent should set for himself three objectives: suitable library facilities for every school; a trained librarian for every library; and a teacher in every classroom who utilizes the services of the library and librarian.
>
> The superintendent is responsible for securing the librarian; there will be none unless one is employed and none will be elected unless the superintendent makes the nomination. . . .
>
> The superintendent may influence the attitude of teachers toward library service. . . .

He may see to it that inservice training orients the teacher in the use of the library. . . . The superintendent has the privilege of introducing the teacher to the library where . . . learning materials may be found.[25]

In further conversation, Smith emphasized that every superintendent must have this specific information and good standards. He should see that there are trained librarians in every school, and where there are ten or more teachers there should be a full time person. He emphasized that this is the time to capitalize on the tremendous parent interest in education and libraries. Last, but not least, he added this important note on human relationships: "An administrator should remember to give the librarian a kind word of praise and approval."[26]

Other administrators amplify and corroborate these statements.

". . . the principal must actively support and believe in the library as an important part of the school. He must actively support the library in planning the schedule and school organization; he must take care of the library budget-wise, and continually represent the library in his request to the superintendent of schools for school personnel and supplies. The principal can do a lot to help build up the library materials. His secretary can take some of the clerical chores off of the librarian and make it possible to have a library function. He can get parent interest and assistance in the library by his leadership with the Parent Teacher Association and other parent contacts in the school."[27]

"The attitude and vision of the principal of a school is the key to the success of the library program. He must keep the superintendent and the board of education aware of the needs of the library."[28]

"The administrator should have a concept of what the elementary library program really is and a knowledge of things that could be developed. He should give encouragement to the librarian. He is responsible in helping to motivate interest among faculty to feel the nearness and importance of the facility, in promoting definite understanding that work must be coordinated with the library and in all subject areas."[29]

Another principal reminds his fellow-workers that they have a direct responsibility to emphasize the materials in the library and to point out topics that could be referred to the library for further study, that they must be enthusiastic, and that they should remember to include the library in helping to orient new teachers.[30] Furthermore, "the principal should go into the library and show an active interest in the library. He can also encourage the use of the bookmobile and public library by the children in his school."[31]

An area of particular significance is that of administration and budget. This "determines how the children will live for the next year through the curriculum enrichment materials that come into the school. The selection of personnel is also important. The principal should foster inservice training and orientation to develop library understanding."[32]

A partial but good summarization of these statements may be found in one school system's library manual. This serves as a constant reminder to all school personnel that the administration is concerned with the direct expansion of the service.

Responsibility of the Principal in the Development of the Library Program

To encourage the provision of library
 facilities and resources in the school.
To supervise the securing and maintaining
 of an adequate book collection.

To know the resources available in the school library and to encourage teachers to use them.
To make it possible for all teachers to utilize library resources in their classroom programs.
To help the librarian and teachers integrate the library program with the total school program.
To coordinate the school's library program with the library program of the county (or other system).
To evaluate periodically the success of the library program.
To interpret the library program to the community and to solicit the community's assistance in its improvement.[33]

To the above may be added these further responsibilities deduced from the comments of the administrators:

To work with teachers and librarians to plan an integrated program of library instruction.
To provide an adequate library staff.
To encourage the use of the library for reading guidance as well as for curriculum enrichment.

Administrative Ideas for Expansion

These administrators were asked also for suggestions which might prove of assistance to those people in other school systems who might be interested in starting or expanding an elementary school library program. These are some positive techniques which may be put into action according to the various school situations.

"An administrator must reach out to other

administrators to help them to have a better appreciation of teaching and library relationships. A keen administrator who can properly present the program is essential. He should attend discussion groups and conferences and should give himself contacts with some of the enthusiastic people in the field."[34] "The best way to convince other administrators is by taking them to visit a good school library in full swing."[35]

"To develop a library program the superintendent should try to find one school interested in such a program. If it can be demonstrated that a good school library is a valuable asset to the educational program in that school the idea will spread to other schools. There is a great need to educate school boards and administrators in the advantages of good school libraries. Such education could very well take place during the programs of state, regional, and national groups of superintendents and school board associations. The leaders in the library field should offer their services to those groups toward this end."[36] In the same way a "principal who believes in libraries can have an active role in encouraging other principals to support and build their own libraries to provide wide and extensive materials for children. This can be done through individual contacts, professional writings, professional organizations. This might also be done through planned contacts within the local school system. He can help sell his superintendent on the role of the library, obtain library appropriations, etc. . . He can constantly bring to the attention of parents and children the local services available through the local community, county or state. . . . As a member of a service club, he has also some responsibility in getting these organizations to work for constructive educational and library programs in the community."[37]

"It is very important to interest your board of education. Run a workshop for members to introduce some of the new educational ideas including the library program. Show actual libraries in operation to the sceptics. Some effort should be made to establish in colleges a course or similar means to help administrators develop understanding of the library program, to indicate their specific responsibilities."[38]

It is evident then that advertising plays a basic part in this phase of the public relations program of the school. "Sell the program to the community first. Parents will demand it from their boards of education. Parents that read and have had some library experiences will push it for their children. Administrators must also be educated to appreciate, understand and work for the elementary school library program."[39]

"The problem lies with the public. We must sell the people on the idea of what constitutes a library, the type of books and materials; who selects them and why. Parent education is so vital."[40]

Administrators believe, therefore, that there are several important emphases which are necessary to the achievement of good elementary school library programs. These include such facets as: (1) training for librarians in the fields of child growth and development and curriculum needs; (2) encouraging library-centered methods of teaching in the courses for elementary teachers; (3) publicizing to other administrators the values of library service; (4) emphasizing the specific administrative responsibilities in this area of the elementary school program.

References

1. Thomas G. Pullen, Jr., State Superintendent of Schools. Take a Look At Our School Libraries. Board of Education of Baltimore County, Towson, Maryland, 1956. n.p. (Processed).

2. Gordon F. Anderson, Administrative Assistant to the Superintendent, District No. 65, Evanston, Illinois.

Role of the School Administrator 167

3. C. Ward, Principal, Stearman School, Wichita, Kansas.
4. Mrs. Ruth Henson, Principal, Dodson School, Fulton County, Georgia.
5. George F. Johnston, Principal, Campfield School, Baltimore County, Maryland.
6. M. G. Bowden, Principal, Casis School, Austin, Texas.
7. Clarice C. Agnew, Principal, Euclid School, Jamestown, New York.
8. Benjamin L. Smith, formerly Superintendent of Schools, Greensboro, North Carolina.
9. Carrie Phillips, Principal, Brooks School, Greensboro, North Carolina.
10. Eva Mae Ivey, Principal, Parklande School, Fulton County, Georgia.
11. Violet Gilman, Principal, Alpharetta School, Fulton County, Georgia.
12. Mary J. Thompson, Principal, Hammond Elementary School, Fulton County, Georgia.
13. Robert J. Shockley, Principal, Loch Raven School, Baltimore County, Maryland.
14. Alnetia K. Ewing, Vice Principal, Curriculum Coordinator, Oakleigh School, Baltimore County, Maryland.
15. Jeanne Brouillette, Curriculum Coordinator, District No. 65, Evanston, Illinois.
16. Loretta Doyle, Assistant Coordinator of Curriculum, District No. 65, Evanston, Illinois.
17. Op. cit., Anderson.
18. Op. cit., Smith.
19. Ailene Beeson, Principal, Archibald D. Murphey School, Greensboro, North Carolina.

20. Op. cit., Shaw.
21. Op. Cit., Ivey.
22. Op. cit., Shockley.
23. Philip J. Weaver, Superintendent of Schools, Greensboro, North Carolina.
24. Oscar M. Chute, Superintendent of Schools, District No. 65, Evanston, Illinois.
25. Benjamin Lee Smith, "Nerve Center: The School Library," The School Executive, LXXVII:55-7, October, 1957.
26. Op. cit., Smith.
27. Op. cit., Bowden.
28. Op. cit., Chute.
29. Neill A. Bridges, Principal, East Point Elementary School, Jamestown, New York.
30. C. Walter Alexis, Principal, Clinton V. Bush School, Jamestown, New York.
31. Op. cit., Thompson.
32. Arthur E. Hamalainen, Principal, Plandome Road School, Manhasset, New York.
33. The Elementary School Library, Office of the Supervisor of School Libraries, Baltimore County Schools, Towson, Maryland. (Mimeographed).
34. Op. cit., Smith.
35. Op. cit., Shockley.
36. Op. cit., Chute.
37. Op. cit., Bowden.
38. Op. cit., Hamalainen.
39. Joseph T. Barlow, Principal, Oakleigh School, Baltimore County, Maryland.
40. Op. cit., Ivey.

Chapter VIII
Auxiliary Features

Although this discussion of the elementary school library program does not include specific methods for technical processes or details of organization and administration, there are certain mechanics connected with good school library service which are of significance. Publicity, scheduling, student assistant organization, media services and library quarters support the program of curriculum enrichment and reading for pleasure. Without these, the purposes of the elementary school library are only partially achieved.

Publicity

The Madison Avenue cult has certain attributes in common with elementary school librarians. Both are advertisers and both are constantly searching for the unusual, the exhibit or the slogan that will attract the largest clientele to a particular service. The need for variety, the need to capitalize on the interest of the moment, the need to publicize to a varied group of people (in this case, teachers, students and parents) and the need to focus attention on a pertinent idea are basic to library publicity.

Bulletin boards, display cases, corridor exhibits, posters, bulletins and letters, Book Week, Book Fairs, Spring Book Festivals, visits from authors and illustrators, radio and TV programs are used to market the services of the elementary school library. All these stimulate interest in reading and serve to display the creative works of children, to indicate new materials to teachers, to share the pleasures of children's books with parents and to educate in library skills.

Display and bulletin boards. One of the simplest methods to help justify the library's role as the center of the school is to display the children's own work, particularly those things that result from using the library. The culmination of a unit of study, such as a second grade's fascinating collection of seeds all carefully cataloged and labelled, is of interest and value to the whole school and can be shared through the library. Displays featuring hobbies of children, tying them in with library materials, help the students identify themselves with the library program.

One rather unusual display, which caused a good deal of comment, was labelled "Then and Now." Paper dolls, arithmetic books, primers, sixth-grade readers and social studies books from the early 19th century were compared with modern day counterparts. The contrasts and similarities were amazing and stimulated the circulation of books about "old things."[1] Illustrations prepared by a third grade for the "Twelve Days of Christmas" provided a charming bit of decoration for the library and, used with the record, delighted the entire school for days.[2]

One librarian posted a schedule of corridor exhibits for the year in the library. Committees from the fourth, fifth and sixth grade rooms sign up for two week displays and indicate the subject or theme they wish to use. These choices are made by the children. The librarian merely checks for duplication. The only stipulation is that it must relate to library material. Themes such as early pioneers, animals, winter reading, American authors, future in space and automobiles are very popular.[3]

Other librarians encourage their student assistants to help plan bulletin boards. Occasionally a librarian will turn over a bulletin board to one grade and the various rooms will take turns sharing information, pictures, etc. which come as a result of their social studies or science units. A short bibliography posted with the display may be made by the librarian, but it is more effective if chosen by the children from the books which seem important to them.

Bulletin boards which display original illustrations from favorite books, from a second grade's interpretation of Little Bear to a sixth-grader's Junket, always renew interest in these books. Even the simplest ideas can be effective. "Good Books for Wise Owls," which featured a paper bag owl's head and a collection of book jackets, was colorful but not elaborate, nor did it take a great deal of the librarian's time.[4]

One rather choice bulletin board was created by a fifth grade girl. Against a crayon background of undersea life full of fish shapes, shells and seaweed, she had displayed book jackets, both fiction and non-fiction relating to the sea, and in the center placed an intriguing bit of original verse.[5]

One other bulletin board should be mentioned here because it attempted to arouse interest at home in the child's reading. Entitled, "To Share With Your Family," a collection of book jackets from favorite read-aloud stories was centered around a splendid picture of a father and son sharing Treasure Island. The librarian achieved a three-dimensional effect by using long portrait pins, and a modernistic touch by connecting all jackets and the picture with colored yarn in such a way as to suggest the shape of a house.[6]

Miscellanies. Articles advertising a book fair, a Book Week program or other special library events, "New Books" reviewed by the librarian or by children for the school paper or the local newspaper, radio and TV programs calling attention to these and other library services--all of the usual advertising devices may be used just as effectively by the elementary school librarian as in any other field. One school system presents a simple radio program each year which may include a story hour and a discussion on how the library helps the reading program.

Favorite book characters made of clay or papier-mâché or with book jacket faces and folded construction paper clothes may be found on tables or perched on book shelves. Art teachers are glad to help create these characters or to give guidance for effective bulletin boards. The techniques which the children themselves learn--Hallowe'en masks, paper bag puppets, stitchery, torn paper designs--are all effective and even the most unartistic school librarian can easily adapt them for her purposes.

From one sixth grade room came mobiles. Some of them illustrated one book such as White Stag, others a collection of favorite characters such as Maid Marian, The Three Bears, and Black Beauty.[7]

Original book jackets designed by the children with a picture to illustrate a favorite scene, a "blurb," and information about the author are not only effective book report devices but, when displayed in the library, are a far better advertisement for the book than a librarian's "I think you will like this one."

Letters and bulletins to teachers. Many librarians employ an open letter to teachers to acquaint them with library news. A library letter may contain hints on "How do you encourage reading," or a note on the coming inventory dates. It may be a welcoming letter in the fall of the year reminding teachers and students of the objectives of the library program, the rules for circulation, some of the special services. One librarian sends out fairly regularly Library Doin's which might include reminders about story hours, thoughts on a recent library conference, or a note about the new children's librarian in the public library.[8]

A service which may legitimately come in this

category, although more specifically classified as a teaching aid, is a monthly list distributed by one librarian. "Come into the library and browse. Perhaps the following magazine articles will be helpful to you and your class. They are available for the asking." Among the headings in this list are "Social Studies," "Science," "Art," "Articles of Interest To All." The article is listed by title, magazine and issue. The teachers in this school mentioned this service many times.[9]

In one large school system the librarians appointed an editorial committee and Charging Out, covering professional news, aids and general information, circulated regularly among the librarians.[10]

Parent-librarian relationships are discussed elsewhere, but it should be remembered that letters to parents and talks to Mothers Groups and the P.T.A. are also important facets of the library publicity program.

Book Week, Spring Book Festivals, book fairs. All through this study it is evident that children, teachers and librarians enjoy sharing books, and now, more and more parents are participating as well. Assembly programs and book fairs encourage fathers and mothers to come and listen, to observe and learn.

Book Week programs are planned by the librarians, the student assistants, the teachers and their classes. Sometimes they are based on the theme of a current Book Week poster. Occasionally they are based on a favorite book, such as a dramatization of Wicked John and the Devil; they may present a discussion of Newbery Award books, as a fourth grade's panel on White Stag, The Voyages of Dr. Dolittle, Daniel Boone, Strawberry Girl and King of the Wind,[11] they may refer to the proper care of books. Occasionally these programs are produced on the local radio or TV stations.

Many librarians plan to have a children's author, illustrator or a visiting story teller during Book Week. In one school the librarian tells stories each morning of Book Week over the school's "intercom."[12] The Junior Chamber of Commerce in another community loans its display case on the city's "four corners" to the schools for Book Week purposes.[13] National Library Week also has become a popular time for such exhibits. A spring Book Festival, presented the first day of spring by a group of third-graders, was a direct outgrowth of some poetry appreciation sharing in the library.[14]

Book fairs are becoming more and more popular, and in many schools the librarian and the P.T.A. sponsor them together. It is an excellent way to present to the parents the new and better books as well as the old favorites, and the children make wonderful publicity agents. The one danger here lies in an overeagerness "to make money." Quantity thus results in a lack of quality in the books being exhibited. Surely this is an opportunity to display the best that is available for children, rather than to promote a money-raising scheme.

It is apparent that most of these devices stem directly from work which the teachers and librarian continually carry on in the area of reading guidance and literary appreciation. But whatever the source of the program, whatever the device employed, each librarian must find the most effective means, individually or collectively, for selling her wares within her school community.

Schedules

The debate over scheduling or not scheduling classes for regular library periods in the elementary school is still evident. Some of the many arguments which have been presented for both sides are discussed here in relation to the schools visited. The major-

Auxiliary Features

ity of the librarians visited are of the opinion that flexible scheduling is an absolute necessity in today's educational program. But others continue to insist that scheduling on a part-time basis is the only way to ensure continual contact with all teachers and students.

In systems where every class is scheduled once or twice a week, according to administrative directives, the work of the limited library staff was handicapped. Little time was allowed for the librarian to perform the preparatory work that keeps a program going. Nor was there time for the librarian to work on special projects, to invite a class to return to the library to continue some research in which they had become interested, to encourage a group to come to enjoy a special story or poetry hour, or even to have simply enough available time for those students with individual needs and curiosities for whom the library should be the obvious source of answers. In such situations some librarians have found it expedient to use one period for checking and browsing and the other in pursuit of information. This demands special planning by teacher and librarian.

On the other hand, in schools where no attempt whatever is made to provide for groups or individuals to come to the library regularly or to note which teachers are or are not taking advantage of the opportunity to follow through on the needs that may have arisen in the classroom study, there is some danger that children may be deprived of library experiences. Shy children or slow readers may be thrust aside by the more aggressive ones. Adequate use of the unscheduled library program means that the librarian must plan constantly with her teachers, make suggestions about materials available in the units being studied, provide story hours and browsing periods which will attract the children to the library, be aware of the needs of special children, keep track in her own plan book of the groups coming regularly and the specific use made of library facilities. She must be sure that all of the facilities and services which are guaranteed through a semi-scheduled program will assuredly be made available to all students in her school. In the non-scheduled programs many teachers also check on their class visits to the library insuring a reasonably regular program of visitation.

The flexible schedules which many librarians prefer make it possible for the librarian to reserve certain periods every day for open reference work so that a teacher may plan to bring her group in for special work as the need arises. It means that sudden and immediate curiosities also may be satisfied and need not be pushed aside because "the library is closed to our group today." It means that a teacher may send one of her reading groups to the library for guided free reading while working with other groups in her room and know that the librarian will be available. It means that classes may be shifted around to fit special library needs. It means that the librarian may visit in the classroom to observe how materials are being used and to have a better understanding of the teaching program.

Many patterns have been worked out to provide the maximum use of the library. For example, in one school the 9-10 hour is for special group time. A teacher may request that hour and the librarian can schedule it specifically knowing that a special need has arisen, e.g., special reference work with library tools for a sixth grade.[15] Some librarians post the weekly schedule on the library door for quick reference by all; others put it on the bulletin board in the library office. In one system the librarian devised forms for the teachers in grades 1 and 2, 3 and 4, 5 and 6. These are distributed to the teacher in quantity at the beginning of the year and are turned in on the last day of the week. The date and the teacher's name are followed by a series of questions or statements relating to the type of library activity which the teacher wishes to have in the library that week. These forms were designed with the teacher so that all types of activities, materials and suggestions could be easily identified.[16]

When planning the library schedule it is essential that the teacher and the librarian understand the purpose of the library program. It is not necessary to teach aloud every time a class visits the library. Browsing periods are as essential as planned instruction. The story hours, the research periods, the periods for teacher and pupil browsing, the scheduled or unscheduled class hours should be used to their fullest extent by all concerned.

An interesting experimental program was developed in one school where principal, teachers and librarian agreed that "when the librarian's time was tied up with a whole class each period of the school day we were not keeping the library in focus with the needs of the rest of the school." The experimental plan had blocks of time available to all classes for practicing skills taught and for individual research. Reading guidance periods were scheduled for books and reading. Teacher-librarian conferences scheduled before school every morning gave time for planning the individual classroom needs. During the block periods, individuals, small groups and/or whole classes could use the library. At the end of the first year, the staff was enthusiastic. After three years one teacher summarized the strengths of flexibility: "Children are having a great opportunity to investigate this library. I think that they are using the various extras of the library-- special research sources, picture files, magazines and newspapers. Children are able to use the library to answer questions as these questions are raised in the classroom instead of waiting for 'their period.' My students are using more library materials. It encourages independence and reliability." With some perception she added, "Perhaps the greatest weakness is the demand put upon the librarian herself in this type of program. The children and teachers are so enthusiastic about it, that perhaps we all take advantage of our librarian!"[17]

Many of the librarians in the larger elementary schools have found it helpful to request that library books should be returned the first hour in the morning of the day on which they are due. This enables them to make better use of their student assistants and to have the books available for the regularly scheduled classes which follow. Special requests or personal reserves may be handled more easily in this way. Naturally there is much leeway allowed here. Books which are to be used that day for a special report, a story that isn't quite finished, a point that needs to be checked with the teacher are all legitimate reasons for waiting until later in the day to return the book. Obviously, of course, a child may return his books and check out others at any time that he desires. But it is most important that the librarian should not allow her eagerness for smooth routines to stifle the child's eagerness to make complete use of his book.

It is generally acknowledged that children should be able to come into the library at any time to exchange books or work on reports, providing they do it quietly and without disturbing the librarian if she is busy with another group. It is obvious, of course, that the library should be large enough to seat one class comfortably with room to spare for individuals and small committees. New libraries should be planned with this in mind.

It is important to note that all classes from kindergarten on should be included. It is not sound to rationalize that the younger the child the less need there is for him to have library experiences. The first introduction to books, the first reading experiences are the foundation for all future pursuits of knowledge. When a class of first- or second-graders is receiving special instruction on circulation procedures or on how to locate their books, the librarian may find it helpful to reserve a series of periods for this instruction when other groups will not interrupt.

Some librarians schedule browsing periods the last hour in the afternoon. This is particularly valuable in rural areas or large centralized schools where the majority of the school population is dependent upon bus transportation. It is also helpful for the eager readers who need another book or the curious ones who are still asking questions. This period is not intended, however, to be used as a "dumping ground" for the problem child who is not interested in the class activities, or for the one who has finished his work and has become a nuisance to the teacher. It goes without saying that all libraries should be open before and after school for informal use and to satisfy the reading needs of any child in the school.

As the library experience thus becomes one of the basic ingredients in the teacher's daily classroom planning, it becomes less necessary for the librarian to pin down each class to a specific visit. The less structured or tightly scheduled the library program is, the more comprehensive is the service which it can give, with this added premise, that the librarian still retains the responsibility of seeing that all are served equally and adequately. Flexibility therefore gives freedom of choice to all.

Student Assistants

"The highest of distinctions is service to others."
King George V, May 1937 [18]

The student assistant program in the elementary school library is a rather nebulous one from the point of view of organization but is very strong in its informal existence. Many a school librarian will testify that the elementary boys and girls are far more efficient and eager helpers in the library than are the older students.

Most librarians have found that the best plan is to use student help before and after school, or perhaps during the noon hour, rather than to try to have regular scheduled assistance throughout the day. One teacher who believes that being a library helper is a valuable learning experience allows those who wish to help to go to the library at about twenty-minute intervals during the afternoon; when one signs in, the next signs out. The only stipulation made is that one does not go to the library if a review or check up is being given in class. Of course, if class work suffers, the privilege is withdrawn.[19] There are occasions, too, when teachers may feel that it is wise for a particular child to be excused from class to help in the library. But, generally speaking, the program of teaching in the elementary grades today excludes the use of released time for library assistance during regular classes.

There are valid exceptions to the above statement, however, and they include an area of therapy. Children react very differently in varying environments and with certain people. It is this fact which has motivated teachers to suggest that certain so-called problem children be given a chance to help in the library. It may be simply the need for a job with responsibility--a chance for the child to prove that he can be of service to the school. It may be a child who is a slow reader, as compared with the rest of his grade, who has thus become a behavior problem. In one school just such a lad in the fourth grade was given the opportunity to help the librarian each morning. At first, able to do only the simplest straightening of shelves, he graduated in a few weeks to shelving easy and picture books. Suddenly one morning the librarian realized that activity had ceased. A quiet search led to B--- in a corner on the floor reading a primer. Needless to say, he was not disturbed. But the opportunity shortly presented itself for the librarian and B---to discuss when to read and when to work. A mutual agreement was reached. B---continued to help his friend the librarian and at the same time discovered that reading could be fun. Tested at the end of the year, he showed a gain of two grades in his reading ability.[20]

Auxiliary Features

In another school a sixth-grade girl with a much lower mental age came in every day to help the librarian deliver the movies to the classrooms, sort out the audio-visual requests and generally tend the desk. Her enthusiasm for the job betrayed her need for recognition among her peers. She was completely at home with the librarian and talked over many of her problems with her. In this way the librarian, without appearing to betray confidences, was able to work with the guidance counselor toward achieving security for the youngster.[21]

Most of the student library helpers are alert, active and eager users of library materials. They are the ones who help do many of the routine tasks, who can help out when the librarian is called from the room. They often give assistance when the primary children come to the library and serve as wonderful liaison people between the library and the classroom. Many librarians have found that from third grade on, the children all clamor for a chance to "stamp out" the books. This job, which often leads to the development of regular assistants, is passed right down the alphabetical class list. These student library helpers should not be confused with the "room librarians" who help the teacher take care of the library books which are in the classroom for long periods.

The Library Squad in one school includes fourth- and fifth-graders. Ten people whom it would benefit most are chosen from each room, with the teacher helping to guide the selection. The helpers work from 8 to 9 A.M. usually, although one-half hour near the end of the day at the convenience of the teacher is occasionally given. The group of helpers rotates each week by room. Five areas of activities are included: housekeeping, desk work, new books, library service, and publicity and exhibits. All are duties which the children can execute themselves without continual supervision and are, of course, rotated among the squad. A "Certificate of Service" is presented at a school assembly in the spring of the year.[22]

This next program employs a somewhat different organization. One group of students helps in the library before and after school, two each time, to file cards, count circulation and take care of the before school rush. The other group is composed of three from each class with the following duties: one opens and sorts the books returned that hour; the second cards; the third charges out the new books. The first two also help to shelve. This arrangement rotates among the three helpers. This program includes all classes from second grade through sixth. The only exception is that second- and third-graders do not shelve nonfiction. The librarian conducts a training program in the fall, and the assistants are recognized with certificates at a special assembly. One assistant explained what it meant to her to be a helper.

Library Helper

When you are a Library Helper you are working with many different kinds of friends. As you card and stamp each book you learn something new by its title.

Library helping may be hard work to some people, but when you like to read books it's an easy task. When you put the books on the shelf in their proper places, it is fun to glance at the titles of the books next to the one you are putting away.

It has been a lot of fun watching our library grow from 3,000 books five years ago to 6,913 books at the present date. Three years ago the library helpers took a trip to the Book Bindery.

Since I have been a library helper I have learned to look up books in the card catalog. This will help me in all the rest of my school years. I like my job being a library helper very much. It has taught me to believe the saying, "A book is a person's best friend."[23]

Still another type of program developed is the Library Council. Rather similar to the Student Council, it consists of representatives from each classroom who meet regularly to help develop good library citizenship both in the library and in the classroom. They also have their own book programs, aid in the Book Week preparations, perhaps sponsor an author or present a special assembly program.

Whatever the form of organization or the hours of work, the reward is primarily in the joy which the elementary child so easily finds in doing a good job and being of service in his school. The recognition with a pin or a certificate in a school assembly for the library aides is of secondary importance. As one librarian said, "My teachers understand the value of regular library assistants before and after school as well as during those fifteen-minute periods in school time. They recognize that children love to help in the library. It makes them feel important and needed."[24]

Student assistants are of immense help to the librarian. A well planned program for the assistant can do much to lighten some of the tasks which often cause a librarian, constantly in need of more clerical assistance, to bog down. It should be clearly understood, however, that this is in no way a substitute for regular paid clerical assistance. An adult assistant brings continuity, rapidity, understanding and maturity to a job which cannot be expected from the elementary child and which is of more worth over a long period of time. The student library assistance program must be planned in such a way that it will not exploit the child but rather teach library values. Furthermore, lasting values can accrue only in situations where the librarian has time to guide and to supervise the children. Pride in achieving a high standard of work even though routine, the development of the sense of responsibility, the library learnings, the therapeutic values in the areas of behavior and reading problems are all potent arguments for further expansion of this facet of librarianship in the elementary school.

Media Services

Throughout this survey, the basic concept of the elementary school library as a complete media center has been emphasized. It may be useful at this point, however, to elaborate on some of the special services and programs in the non-print area which make today's school libraries different from those of ten years ago.

The problem-centered method of teaching, with its emphasis on independent individual study, plus the innate curiosities of boys and girls have increased the complexity of the task of the teacher. A good teacher realizes she is not effective until all students enjoy and profit by their learning experiences. The choice of appropriate, multi-media, instructional aids often creates the difference between success and failure in the classroom. The elementary school librarian has a responsibility to help teachers select and utilize these materials. All the schools consider as a minimum the inclusion of filmstrips and slides, transparencies, models and specimens, records and tapes, pictures (mounted or framed), plus the equipment needed to use these. In addition, many schools include 8mm films as well as the familiar 16mm, graphics in many forms, programmed instruction devices, and occasionally video tape cameras, closed circuit TV, and dial access tape disks. Carrels or tables for listening and viewing are found in all libraries.

The organization of such material varies according to the space and facilities available and the processing decisions made by the local system. Various codes (color and mnemonic) are used in cataloging, but all cards are filed in the regular catalog so that teachers and students have immediate retrieval access to

Auxiliary Features

all materials. A production center as a part of the media suite is included in many of the new buildings, for both teachers and students are involved in this activity. Transparencies, single concept films and tapes are among the aids regularly created to supplement teaching and other sharing techniques. Children summarize their reports, report field trips, prepare book reports for future use on tape.

ETV science lessons are used widely and librarians supplement these in many ways. Science book trucks, which include print and other media relating to the current unit and of various reading levels, are popular because they give every child something to do or to experiment on. Teachers check out the science trucks as desired. Librarians must therefore be alert to programs being viewed and knowledgeable about the lessons in advance in order to have sufficient materials. Some librarians serve on the TV planning committees in order to aid with materials selection.

Primary children particularly enjoy record/tape and slide combinations. They can manipulate the equipment themselves and benefit from being able to repeat as they desire. They move easily into this type of individual instruction. Transparencies are also favored by this age group "because they're fun to make and show what I want to tell." Transparencies made by a mothers' group to illustrate storybook characters were popular in one school. Volunteers also make many of the storytelling tapes for individual use or for dial access decks, since appropriate ones are not available in large quantity commercially. Centralized production of tapes is available in many systems. The master tape is kept on file and librarians in any school may order for their own collections.

One librarian kept a quantity of grease pencils, kleenex and reclaimed X-ray film at the circulation desk. Children could make their own transparencies in the library and view them on the projector there.

Second-graders' notes on fish and amphibians were most original![25]

Dial access stations in libraries and/or classrooms in the elementary program are just beginning to be installed. The listening booths in one media center number twelve, and the children have access to approximately 120 different programs. This service is again significant for individual instruction: children may listen to poetry and music, may get help in English or a foreign language, may listen to a folktale relating to their social studies, or may hear repeats of guest lecturers in their schools. This is an educational technology development which will grow in use and make the media center even more of an extension to the classroom.

Likewise, listening stations serve several teaching purposes: for example, to teach readiness for reading skills per skill; to give complicated directions for use of equipment, location of library tools; to listen to a story and write one's own ending; to aid in learning how to take notes. Picture books may be viewed while listening to tapes, to "catch the symbol with the sound." This is particularly helpful with slow readers.

An especially interesting ETV series has been developed in one system. "Magic Book" is in two parts, kindergarten through third grade, and fourth through seventh. Books appropriate to these ages are discussed or told. The weekly outline includes a short booklist of related stories for each presentation. Each series is scheduled for four times a week so that a teacher may time it when it best fits into the classroom program. Occasionally teachers will supplement the series with other stories or with discussions, planned or spontaneous.[26] A similar program, "The Magic Book Shelf," is produced in another system and is designed to encourage reading all types of literature and to emphasize the role of the school library as the source of many instructional materials.[27]

The many familiar audio-visual aids--flannel boards, maps, globes, community and family resource files, field trips--play a significant role in the media center and should continue to be included when planing this phase of the collection. In almost all schools, children are being permitted to check out the A-V aids just like books. The children are relatively familiar with most of the equipment and, indeed, handle the material with much greater ease than many classroom teachers. Although books will continue to be the most intimate kind of viewing experience, all media is significant in today's world and learning the art of listening and viewing is a part of the instructional program.

Physical Quarters

The physical appearance of the media center is important. The library must have a congenial welcoming atmosphere. A large part of this stems from that elusive quality, the librarian's personality, but selection of equipment and careful planning help. The room should be attractive, well lighted and spacious. There should be corners for story hours and other group activities. It should contain comfortable furniture, scaled for kindergarteners as well as sixth-graders, and good work tables and carrels, efficiently arranged for study and reference. Space should be provided for working tools such as the card catalog or audio-visual equipment, as well as for technical processing needs and storage. Colorful drapes or curtains, plants, good works of art, display space, bulletin boards, even aquariums may add to the charm and individuality of the room.

In both old and new buildings a central location for the library has usually been planned. In the instances where this was not done or where there was an inefficient layout, it has been due to a lack of opportunity for consultation on the part of the librarian with the architect and administrator.

In most areas where elementary school buildings are rapidly being built, the library supervisors have prepared a formula for their school architects. The space is equipped as a media center from the start to avoid being taken over for classrooms even on a temporary basis, and includes work rooms with running water, storage facilities, supply cabinets, work space, record and filmstrip cabinets, equipment storage, and production facilities.

Almost every library visited, either old or new, was large enough to contain a class at work plus small groups from other rooms. In the few places where this service was curtailed, the librarian commented feelingly about the loss in use of materials which inevitably resulted. Inadequate shelving was a usual accompaniment to this problem.

Exciting and interesting uses are being made of color in both new and old libraries. One remodelled room, using light maple shelving, had light blue walls and dusty pink window frames. The ceiling had been lowered with acoustical blocks and fluorescent lighting added. Beige colored formica top tables in hexagonal and oblong shapes were combined with posture chairs in pink fiberglass. An 8' x 10' beige rug in one corner made an attractive story hour setting.[28] In another remodeled building a charming wallpaper patterned the high walls above the painted shelving and cafe curtains were used in the long windows. Flame and gray green are the eye-catching color combination in one new library.

A multi-purpose room was converted into a media center in one building by a judicious use of varied carpeting and furniture for browsing areas, for storytelling area, for reference study, etc. Color was in evidence. A section with early American furniture set off a reading spot. Vertical files, individual study tables, reference books and viewing-listening carrels occupied another quarter of the room; a large carpeted area with-

Auxiliary Features

out furniture provided space for book discussion group, large story hours. The stage was available for creative dramatics. Materials of all kinds were easily accessible. Youngsters came and went freely. "Here," said the principal, "youngsters can check anything out, from a book to a pickled snake."[29] Some librarians have even aspired to an outside patio for story hours and book sharing time. In all of the libraries a window seat or a rocking chair, hassocks, colorful "sit-upons" or a rug form a group center. Carrels and listening and viewing stations have been included in all centers whether new or remodeled.

To achieve these effects it is not necessary to spend large amounts of money for furnishings. A small amount judiciously applied can create a new atmosphere. Informality is the keynote, combined with the most functional designs and equipment available. Such elementary school libraries are a joy to behold and are obviously used and appreciated by the children and the teachers.

It is evident that certain seasoning ingredients contribute toward an enriched program within the elementary school library. Atmosphere, advertising, student assistants, clerical assistance, audio-visual aids, program arrangements and physical quarters assume a significance of their own in relation to the total program and add proportionately to the services available for students and teachers.

References

1. Congress Park School, LaGrange, Illinois.
2. Washington School, Evanston, Illinois.
3. Ibid.
4. Parklane School, Fulton County, Georgia.
5. Alexander School, Jackson, Tennessee.
6. Timber Ridge School, Evanston, Illinois.

7. College Hill School, Evanston, Illinois.
8. Plandome Road School, Evanston, Illinois.
9. Cossitt School, LaGrange, Illinois.
10. Baltimore County, Maryland.
11. Sternberger School, Greensboro, North Carolina.
12. Napier School, Nashville, Tennessee.
13. Greensboro, North Carolina.
14. Irving Park School, Greensboro, North Carolina.
15. Rock Creek School, Montgomery County, Maryland.
16. District No. 7, Phoenix, Arizona.
17. Mt. Olive, Fulton County, Georgia.
18. Quotation appearing on certificate presented to student assistants at Casis School, Austin, Texas.
19. Timber Ridge School, Evanston, Illinois.
20. Linden School, Oak Ridge, Tennessee.
21. Brooks School, Greensboro, North Carolina.
22. Casis School, Austin, Texas.
23. Loch Raven School, Baltimore County, Maryland.
24. Washington School, Evanston, Illinois.
25. Pleasant View School, Wichita, Kansas.
26. Fulton County, Georgia Schools.
27. Houston, Texas Schools.
28. Washington School, Evanston, Illinois.
29. Stearman School, Wichita, Kansas.

Chapter IX
Community Relationships

The direct lines of communication and service between librarian, administrator, teacher and student are supplemented by the working relationships which the librarian has with the parents in her school community, the Parent Teacher Association, the program of the public library in the area and the various other social and community agencies working with her students. All of these groups make definite contributions to the school's program, and in turn, the elementary school librarian offers specific services to them.

Parent Relationships

A discussion of the relationship between the elementary school librarian and the parents in the community divides itself rather broadly into two parts: (1) assistance which parents give to the library, either individually or through the Parent Teacher Association; (2) assistance which the librarian gives to the parents.

Assistance from parents. In many schools there is organized parent help for library clerical assistance. The librarians in these schools feel that it is invaluable. Not only does it free the librarian for more professional service, but it demonstrates the worth of the library program to the parent. It may also result in parents stimulating interest in their own children's use of books and libraries. This service is organized frequently by the chairman of the P.T.A. library committee.

One chairman explained her program in detail. About twenty mothers work twice a month for a couple of hours each to cover the library schedule. Many of the parents chosen are from the primary rooms, since this usually means a longer carry-over in the aide program. A morning coffee meeting is planned to organize the schedule and discuss the program. The librarian explains all the files, sources and library processes which they will be expected to use. This orientation is necessary. Most of the usual clerical jobs are undertaken, and a special effort is made to have one or two typists on the committee. Those especially interested in mending observe the public library's program in this field. The parents also serve during the librarian's absence. This enthusiastic chairman believes that parents can make an important contribution to the school program. The librarian honors these parent assistants at the same assembly honoring her student helpers.[1]

The P.T.A. chairman in another school gives much of her own time as an assistant. She works at her own convenience about two or three days a week and the amount of assistance from parents is at least three full days. The parent assistant helps cut, mount and label, following the librarian's subject heading, the pictures and pamphlets. Occasionally she gives assistance in typing and processing or gathering materials for a teacher's special request under the librarian's supervision.[2]

Another school, through its P.T.A. organization, regularly schedules two parents two days a week in the library. They are trained at the beginning of the year to help process new books, organize audio-visual materials, type Wilson cards (but no actual cataloging) and give other assistance as needed.[3]

One school, the grades of which were taught in several places prior to the opening of the new building, received a tremendous boost from the parents who wanted to insure a library for their children. For nine months prior to the official opening, parents regularly drove, some as far as sixteen miles, to help the librarian process the books. A parent committee still helps at least one afternoon a week to check lists, type cards and do other jobs as needed.[4]

Community Relationships 193

In several other schools the chairman of the library committee gives once a week clerical assistance herself, although there may be no organized help. A particularly nice "thank you" was extended by one librarian with a tea held to honor the "Library Mothers" of her school.

There are some arguments against this type of assistance. Parents may come to feel that they have a right to govern book selection and programs. Said one librarian, "Try not to have officious parents and try for consistent help, perhaps even a carry-over of one or two mothers a year. It is better to have less help, and to be sure it is consistent and accurate."[5] There must be a clear understanding with parent assistants of the librarian's professional responsibility. Furthermore, administrators may not provide regular clerical assistance if volunteer work is easily obtained. The need to free the librarian from the uncertainty of the volunteer schedule and of the constant orientation of new assistants and the need to insure complete coverage of all nonprofessional tasks are fundamental for efficient library service. Nowhere is this more clearly stated than in the new Standards for School Media Programs, which clearly delineates the levels of tasks which should be performed by professional and clerical personnel, the latter employed on a regular basis.

Other valuable services are also carried out by parent groups. One Citizen Advisory Committee is responsible for the Community Resource file, which includes information on possible field trips, individual speakers and special displays. Another organization, feeling that the library plays an important part in encouraging science interests, presented to the library a memorial gift for science books and materials.

Almost every school visited receives some kind of financial assistance from a parent teacher organization. It may be annually or occasionally, but all agree that giving to the library program is one of the best ways of helping all the children in the school.

Various amounts are given and various uses are made of this money. In one school the library received $2,000 the first year of its existence in order to build up the beginning book collection to a basic minimum.[6] In many instances the money is designated for extras which are not available in the regular school library budget. Such "comforts" as cushions for the story hour circle or attractive draperies to control light; special speakers, authors and illustrators for book week programs and assemblies; additional audio-visual materials and magazine subscriptions fall in this category. In several school systems the Parent Teacher Association pays the librarian to keep the library open three mornings a week for six weeks during the summer.

One school system, however, does not encourage the P.T.A. to give regular financial support to the library as a part of their budget. The Board of Education argues that if the library is worth having it should be supported through school board budgetary measures. If the P.T.A. always assisted, the board would not know the library's true needs. The city P.T.A. board agreed to this on condition that the school board would continue adequately to support the library services. Such an understanding does not prevent small occasional gifts to the library, but it does place financial responsibility where it properly belongs.[7] It should be noted that the instances described in the preceding paragraphs are all examples of additional help and that in no school is the library program dependent upon the P.T.A. instead of the regular school budget for its financial existence.

Whatever the gift, it is evident that the library is the recipient because parents are anxious that their library meet the standards of other schools and because they believe that it is basic to the entire school program. One parent actually said, "I'd even be willing to pay higher taxes for this!"

Community Relationships

Assistance to parents. Both elementary school librarians and children's librarians are finding that certain phases of adult education are becoming increasingly their special responsibilities. Introduction of the fine material available in children's books is among the most important of these contributions. One of the areas of interest and cooperative effort between librarian and parents is the Book Fair program. Usually held around Book Week, these fairs may be sponsored jointly by the librarian and the P.T.A. They are intended to present the best of the new books and the most attractive of the old favorites in an effort to show the wealth of children's books on all subjects and on all reading levels, to guide book purchases and to emphasize the building up of home libraries. In some schools, orders are actually taken for these books, and a certain percentage of the money goes to the P.T.A. or library. Many more librarians, however, are finding it wiser to advertise the fair as an exhibit and to distribute book lists which may be used as future guides for purchasing the books. Librarians find it interesting and valuable to make an informal check up after Hanukkah and Christmas to see how many of the children received books, particularly ones chosen at the Book Fair.

Local bookstores are usually most cooperative in supplying books for the display, as are jobbers. Children enjoy helping to organize the display and to man the booths. The librarian's particular responsibility is to insure variety and quality of titles.

Librarians prepare and distribute to parents special lists of many kinds: e.g., home purchases, vacation reading, science and other subjects, read-aloud books. Talks are made at P.T.A. meetings by librarians to encourage family sharing of books. This type of service is second nature to any librarian and the demand for it is as acute in the elementary school as elsewhere.[8]

Another service which is being developed in a good many libraries is the Parent Shelf. This is an attempt to bring together books, brochures and magazines on education and child development as well as official P.T.A. materials which may be of particular interest to fathers and mothers.

A tea with a book display, given by the library committee of one school, presents an opportunity to suggest books which parents might enjoy with their children. This is particularly valuable for parents whose children are just starting in school. The services of the public library are also emphasized. On another occasion in this school a family story hour was presented at a P.T.A. meeting to encourage sharing library books at home. In a similar parent meeting three fathers discussed their favorite books for family use.[9]

A small school in an outlying rural area makes available a selection of adult books which children may take home for their parents.[10] A similar situation exists in a large city school in a low socio-economic area. Here the librarian and the principal emphasize the library program in the hope that the children will talk about books at home, show them and read them to their parents.[11] At Parent Institutes in another school the librarian discusses books to help children in various ways, explains the library program and attempts to build an interest in home libraries.[12]

One librarian always makes sure that the library is open before the P.T.A. meeting. Fathers especially enjoy coming in to browse at that time. A Parent Education shelf is available and at Christmas time special gift suggestions are exhibited.[13] Below is one example of a letter which librarians may send to parents to acquaint them with the special services concerning book selections.

Dear Parents:

As a Book Week project our boys and girls in the fifth and sixth grades were asked to select a book shelf including fifteen books they would most like to include in their own library. A number of students have told me they became so interested in this project that they were asking for books for Christmas this year.

Carefully chosen books may serve as valuable source material, may enhance interest in worthwhile hobbies, and may give endless joy. Most of all, though, book ownership helps immeasurably to instill the love of books in boys and girls--an everlasting joy. As you make your plans for Christmas gifts, won't you include a worthwhile book?

I shall be glad to arrange a conference with you and help in the selection of books for your boy and girl. Attached is a selected list of books on various grade levels and subjects. I have tried to include books that could be enjoyed over a long period of time for I believe that this is an important factor in the selection of books for a personal library.

Merry Christmas.

F-----S-----
Librarian

    Teachers and librarians work closely with the parents to encourage home reading. One fourth grade teacher suggests to parents that they encourage the use of newspapers and magazines for reference work and that they buy books which lead to other books, e.g., biographies of explorers.[14] Other schools suggest to parents that they arrange a place where the child can keep his books. Both teachers and librarians encourage parents to visit bookstores and book fairs with their children to discover their book interests. In this connection, the existence of paperbacks was consistently stressed. There are now good titles published regularly for the elementary age reader. Parents should be introduced to these as supplementary support in building home libraries. Correlated with this type of parent assistance is the effort on the part of librarians to arouse parent interest in unit work. Parents must be helped to realize that library books have as much value as readers and that encyclopedias are not made to be copied for reports. This often leads to broader adult participation, as one boy reported, "My father got so interested in this that he's reading about it now too!" Families are also urged to use special vacation reading lists.

It is most valuable for the librarian to talk with teachers after parent conferences. New insight into home reading habits is gained. Teachers, who ask parents,
> Do you really listen to him read aloud?
> Do you really notice what he brings home on library day? Do you share his books?

and then discuss parent replies with the librarian, help the librarian to offer better reading guidance both at home and at school.

"I wonder what families do that don't read books together. It's like not knowing each other's friends," said the young eight year old in Bequest of Wings.[15] To encourage just exactly this, elementary school librarians frequently prepare special lists for parent's background reading about children's books. One librarian sent home a bulletin entitled:

Why Read

Is reading important?
What do you read?
Does your family enjoy reading a good book together?
Do you give books as gifts to your children?

Community Relationships 199

> Do you know Piglet, Miss Pickerel, Mrs. Goose, Silver Chief, Rufus M and many other modern book characters?
>
> Every child has a regular scheduled library class every two weeks. He may come for reference or additional books before school... at noon... and after school.
>
> There are all types of lists and books available for use in choosing good books to read and buy.
>
> Suggested References:
>
> <u>Bequest of Wings</u> by Annis Duff.
>
> <u>Your Children Want To Read</u> by Ruth Tooze.
>
> <u>The Proof of the Pudding</u> by Phyllis Fenner.
>
> <u>Reading With Children</u> by Anne T. Eaton.[16]

In another community a flyer was prepared for a P.T.A. meeting--"This May Interest You--Your School Library." Under such headings as "A Material Center," "A Reading Center," "Services," "Are School Children Reading," information was succinctly presented. An invitation to ask for guidance in book and encyclopedia purchases concluded the sheet.[17] Still another librarian proposed a brochure, "Reading Aloud in the Home." She discussed the why, how, when and what aspects of this type of sharing, concluding with a series of book reviews of favorite titles. When one parent asked why the emphasis on titles of the past three or four decades, the reply came back "But madam, the children are always new."[18]

"Radio and Television Can Inspire a Child's Love of Reading," states another librarian's note to parents. This is followed by a list of radio and television programs, with time and station, that have proved worthwhile. A postscript calling attention to "The Parent's Bookshelf" in the local paper and the publication, Listenable and Lookables, which screens local educational programs for home and school, was appended.[19]

The following memorandum, which was prepared for distribution to parents during a Book Week celebration by the principal and librarian, again emphasizes the need for establishing a close working relationship between the school library program and the school community.

Some Aims of our Library Program for Boys and Girls:
1. To offer a variety of subjects on all reading levels and to give the "right" book to the "right" child at the "right" time.
2. To teach children to use books and the library to the best advantage.
3. To create in children a love of the beauty in literature so that they may have the wisdom to choose for themselves what is worthwhile.

Suggestions on How Parents May Help the Library to Accomplish its Aims:
1. Encourage the pride of your child in books by helping him to build a worthwhile library for himself at home.
2. Provide a quiet place for your child to read and study so that he may not be distracted by radio and television. Encourage him to have a regular uninterrupted period of study and reading.
3. Encourage your child in the third grade and above to select books he can read and have him read to you. Guard against too frequent readings to your child as he begins to read.
4. Read to your child at a very young age

Community Relationships 201

and when he learns have him read to you, but ask guidance in the selection of appropriate materials. The careful selection of books is of utmost importance to his growth and development.[20]

Librarians, obviously, are keenly aware of the need to develop parental understanding of elementary school library services. And, in those libraries where there is an active program, parent endorsement is vigorous. Their comments speak for themselves:

Mrs. B---, a parent assistant in the library--

> The library has advanced unbelievably. It is the most wonderful thing in the world for the children to use these advantages. They do lots of good research, plus having guided recreational reading. Children have a desire to learn and find out which must be encouraged and developed. The library is a teaching program...and makes a contribution to the whole school program.[21]

A busy P.T.A. officer, Mrs. A---, commented,

> The library is the most important part of our school program. It is important because all small children have a chance to go to the library even though many parents do not take their children to the public library. The P.T.A. makes a financial contribution because the library benefits all children. The community understanding of the library program is solid. The personality of our librarian is important too. She is respected by the whole community.[22]

Mrs. M---had just come in for a parent-teacher conference, but took time to remark,

> I think the elementary school library is wonderful. My two younger ones use it constantly and the two older ones did too when they were here. They get interested in other areas they might not have known about. It is a lure away from constant use of TV. It gives them a sense of independence because they pick out something of their own to take home. It develops responsibility and is a good carry over to use of the public library as well as Junior and Senior High libraries. Books and teaching today are so much more interesting. Children don't say, 'I hate school' anymore. They don't want to miss it![23]

In another community the fourth-grade mothers in one room were delighted to comment on their library.[24]

> The library is just fabulous. Children start at an early age to develop regular patterns of reading and selecting. It's an integral part of education.
>
> There is opportunity to do reference work and work on their own problems. They are well supervised.
>
> The library is a key part of the school program. It guides to new interests.
>
> The library holds everything for all. It is an opportunity to captivate nine year old readers.
>
> We are fortunate to have a librarian who remembers what children know and like . . . brings in other types of books surreptitiously, gives good guidance.
>
> The selection of books is excellent.
>
> This library is not a luxury item.

Reference instigates interest in parents too!

Surely it is evident from such statements that librarians and parents complement each other in the realm of books, children and elementary school library programs.

Public Library Cooperation

Cooperation and understanding between the elementary school librarian and the children's librarian of the public library is important. One can often supplement the other and both are anxious to help the child enjoy his contacts with books and to feel free to use any library resources which are available to him. Both should feel free to suggest to each other ways in which mutual aid can be used advantageously.

Most librarians in the schools observed make a definite effort to let the children's librarian in their community know in advance, whenever possible, what units are about to receive heavy emphasis, to warn her of certain topics for which she may need to reserve materials, and to inform her of the type of question she may be asked. In several schools the children's librarian is invited to visit the school library and give an occasional book talk either in the library or the classroom. This is particularly valuable before the long summer vacation. [25]

During the school year where supplementary bookmobile service is available, children are encouraged to use it. This is true of both city and country programs. In some county schools large collections of books are left as temporary deposits in the elementary school library, particularly in rural areas where reading materials are scarce and in schools where the school library is inadequate. This is much more satisfactory than having the children trooping in and out of the bookmobile at school stops for a limited time. It is a service which is appreciated by both teachers and the school librarian. Children's rooms in public libraries often make long term loans to teachers which help supplement special unit needs.

Visits to the public library and the ownership of borrower's cards are encouraged by both teachers and librarians. Many teachers take their classes during Book Week to see the exhibits and to enjoy the special programs. A first grade teacher takes her class to visit the bookmobile each spring to introduce the summer reading program, the librarian and the schedule, and a letter is sent home with this special information.[26] In another school all grades from four to six annually make a trip to the public library to start their summer reading. Here the school library supplements the public library book collection during the heavy summer influx of readers by lending books from the school library collection.[27]

In some school systems the library is studied in the primary grades as one of the community services. A regular field trip to the nearest branch of the main library is planned for this unit. In the formal program of library instruction, as outlined in another school's language arts guide, the use of the facilities of the public library for both research and recreational reading is emphasized particularly in fifth and sixth grades.[28]

Sparks from the Tinder-Box, the news sheet from the Hans Andersen room of the public library, is posted regularly on one school library bulletin board.[29] The library news sheet in another school headlined the arrival of the new children's librarian in that community's public library. The children's librarian was also invited to be the special story teller during Book Week for this school.[30]

All librarians advertise the vacation reading programs which are sponsored by the public library children's rooms. Many of them recognize the summer readers in a fall school assembly program. The teachers also promote this program with both parents and students. In several communities school and children's librarians work on summer reading lists together as well as on special individual lists. "Adventures in Reading for Boys and Girls," a list for fourth to sixth grades, was sponsored jointly by public and school librarians in one community and distributed widely to parent and teacher groups in the city and around the state.[31] School librarians comment favorably on this carry-over from books in public libraries to books in school libraries. Conversely, the school librarian also may aid the public library's expansion program. A bookmobile stop which was near one school was patronized with great regularity by most of the children. The school librarian capitalized on this to help stir up enthusiasm for a proposed new branch library in that area. Let's Go to the Library by Buchheimer was shared aloud during several library periods, and the librarian talked about the public library and the additional facilities which might come with a new branch. The children's interest in such a project stimulated the adults in the community.[32] Furthermore, in many classrooms children remarked, "I found this at the public library." One child added, "It's so nice to have two libraries, and it's much easier to use the public one now that I've learned how to find books in our own school library."

In one community where the supervisor of children's work is also supervisor of school libraries, there is a very close working relationship and a constant interloan of books to supplement collections and answer emergency calls. This strengthens the understanding of curriculum needs which the public library service also supports, but it may also breed a sense of false economy. Over emphasis of school needs in the public library collection may develop as well as budget complacency on the part of the school board and administration. Both of these tendencies are dangerous to school and public library needs and services.

This interplay of services and collections between school and public library is vital. But it is important to remember that "...the school cannot depend on the public library for its total needs, the school library will lay the foundation for a more extensive use of the public library and a more generous support of its program of service...Both have their places of service and both are entitled to acceptance and support.[33]

Other Community Agencies

In this current period of concern for the inner city child and the culturally deprived child, and with the development of such programs as Operation Headstart and Vista volunteers, it is of even greater importance that the elementary school librarian be aware of and coordinate with the special community agencies. The development of nursery schools in or near the school building, the federal funds available for purchase of materials to help in projects, make it imperative that the librarian open facilities, share knowledge of materials, learn more about the specific children in the program of her neighborhood to help prepare for the transfer and orientation to public school.

The elementary school librarian extends her services to other community agencies as well. She may contribute columns to the city newspaper or send in book reviews by some of the children. Radio and television services have been mentioned previously and the willingness of the librarian to participate in these programs is indicative of her interest in community welfare.

Other activities in which these elementary school librarians participate and which may complement the work of the public librarian, include church and Sunday School libraries; sponsorship for the Junior Red Cross program and interpreter for CARE books; compilation of exhibits and book collections for the community cerebral palsy center; story hours at a school for men-

Community Relationships

tally retarded children. Elementary school librarians work closely with Girl Scout and Boy Scout troops, Brownies, Cubs and Campfire Girls on merit badges and activities, program and handicraft needs. In one library there hangs a painting given by the Girl Scouts in that school as a thank you for the help received in their study of children's illustrators and the "Readers" proficiency badge. Another group of librarians has been working closely with a new Junior Museum in their community, loaning books for special displays and generally advertising its services.[34] Contact is often made with local welfare and social agencies through the school guidance programs for this is a helpful way for the librarian to understand some of the reasons behind the reading problems of her clientele.

It is evident, therefore, that the elementary school librarians' services extend into many areas directly and indirectly connected with the school program. These relationships are additional affirmations to the statement made by one principal, "Our library is the key to our school program."[35]

References

1. Casis School, Austin, Texas.
2. Mitchell School, Fulton County, Georgia.
3. Campfield School, Baltimore County, Maryland.
4. Oakleigh School, Baltimore County, Maryland.
5. Ibid.
6. Loch Raven School, Baltimore County, Maryland.
7. School District No. 65, Evanston, Illinois.
8. <u>Growing Up With Books,</u> an R.R. Bowker publication, is by far the most popular list for distribution to all parent groups.
9. Arbutus School, Baltimore County, Maryland.
10. Hopewell School, Fulton County, Georgia.

11. Jones School, Greensboro, North Carolina.
12. Lincoln School, Jackson, Tennessee.
13. Campfield School, Baltimore County, Maryland.
14. Munsey Park School, Manhasset, New York.
15. Annis Duff. Bequest of Wings. New York, Viking Press, 1944. p. 23.
16. Buffalo Street School, Jamestown, New York.
17. General Green School, Greensboro, North Carolina.
18. Library Department, Wichita Public Schools, Kansas.
19. Baltimore County Schools, Maryland.
20. Sternberger School, Greensboro, North Carolina.
21. Mitchell School, Fulton County, Georgia.
22. Parkview School, Jackson, Tennessee.
23. Fairmount School, Jamestown, Tennessee.
24. Lincoln School, Evanston, Illinois.
25. That this need is clearly recognized also by children's librarians is evidenced in the publication Minimum Standards for Public Library Systems, 1966: "Public, school, and academic libraries should work together to provide coordinated service to students." This is an indication of a mutual desire to make the best service available to all youthful library patrons. American Library Association Public Library Association Standards Committee. Minimum Standards for Public Library Systems, 1966. Prepared by the Standards Committee and subcommittee of the Public Library Association, American Library Association .... Chicago, American Library Association. 1967. p. 21-22.

Community Relationships 209

26. Washington School, Evanston, Illinois.
27. Arbutus School, Baltimore County, Maryland.
28. Jackson, Tennessee.
29. Longfellow School, Royal Oak, Michigan.
30. Plandome Road School, Manhasset, New York.
31. Jamestown School, New York.
32. Casis School, Austin, Texas.
33. Evanston, Illinois.
34. B. L. Smith The School Library and the White House Conference. A reprint of an address at the general meeting of the American Association of School Librarians, Philadelphia, July 4, 1955. Published by the Grolier Society for AASL, p. 18-19.
35. Greensboro School, North Carolina.
36. Orrington School, Evanston, Illinois.

Chapter X
Elementary School Libraries Are Realities

"Today just didn't seem like Monday without our library period."[1] This remark, repeated in a variety of ways by many teachers, is typical of the attitude of faculty in elementary schools where they are enjoying the rich library experiences described in the previous chapters. That this program is a necessity, not a luxury; a reality, not merely an idea; that it has values far beyond the small classroom collection; that it provides a definite learning situation for the entire student body are evident.

"It had seemed to me that we might as well keep our carefully selected, easy reading books in our rooms," said a primary teacher. "However, since a library was established in our school, I have come to see its value. These same books are easily accessible at all times. In fact, our librarian keeps us supplied with well chosen materials. The main value of a school library for young children seems to be that it develops a beginning in the library habit, promotes a feeling for the care of books and furnishes another avenue for meaningful experiences. It creates a sense of belonging to the larger group, 'our school.' The value to children with reading disabilities is hard to estimate. Children no longer feel that books have any grade levels, so they feel willing to choose materials that they can enjoy, are able to read and do much to improve their reading. I am heartily in favor of libraries in elementary schools.[2]

A group of teachers commenting on their center said, "The library period is always tied in with the classroom. It's like a series of chain links. Motivation leads to re-enforcement. Everybody comes through the center in the morning--children and teachers. Whatever the central interest is in the classroom, the activ-

Elementary School Libraries Are Realities

ities relating to it receive support from the library." One teacher added, "Let the children's learning go on without you. Offer them as many experiences as we can and let them develop. You see experts develop in class as the year progresses. Each child has much to give and his enthusiasm is often sparked by the library. We could not teach without our center."[3]

An upper grade teacher indicated that the library taught her children self control and consideration of their fellow pupils. It offered a wealth of opportunity to supplement studies in the classroom. She added, "In order to obtain the greatest efficiency and benefits from the elementary school library, it is necessary to have a full-time librarian. It is she who gives the children the fundamental knowledge and skills for the use of the library. ...In order to give the child a wealth of material to develop and improve his background for present and future use, the elementary library and a full time librarian are a very essential part of the child's life in school."[4]

The comments of the children expressing their appreciation and enjoyment of library services were manifold. Only a few can be shared here, but they too indicate the variety of program and services of this facility.

"It's just like going to a new world when you go to the library," said a sixth-grader, and her classmate added, "I can spread my knowledge." The library gives an "opportunity to read more books you want to read," and, "even if you can't travel, you sure can read about other places." You can find "additional information even if you don't check out a book." "Kids that don't have libraries just aren't as fortunate as we are." "Having it in school makes it easier if you live a long way off, and it's right in the center too." "I just read something so good, it satisfied my appetite. I didn't even know it was lunch time."

Summary of Library Services

It is evident that the librarians in these elementary schools are responsible for many-faceted programs. The librarian must be a professionally trained person with an understanding of library organization, of teaching aids, of elementary curriculum trends, of reading guidance techniques, of all media communication and of the development of elementary children. She must have a sense of critical evaluation as well as personal appreciation of books. She must possess the ability to work easily with many people. She must be able to create a happy environment for human relationships and foster delight in the use of all library materials. Above all, she must be aware of the necessity of a carefully planned program--planned in close cooperation with the teachers and administrators with whom she is working.

This program, then, is a composite one to serve the needs and interests of all grades and of all school personnel. It should include the teaching of library skills and develop appreciation of good books. It should develop an ability in all users to discern the right tools for seeking answers. Opportunities should be provided which will encourage the development of democratic attitudes through library citizenship. The program must be flexible enough to serve the immediate need of the child and the long range planning of the classroom teachers. Awareness of the services which are available in all libraries in various situations should result. These aims are high, and the provision of libraries and librarians who will implement such programs and teachers who can understand and use such facilities is an important part, of the education of young America.

Recommendations for Further Implementation

A survey of this nature inevitably indicates certain requisites for the establishment and continuation

Elementary School Libraries Are Realities

of services. These requisites are not new and may be found in many professional journals. But the fact that they have appeared clearly and consistently in this study makes it obvious that aims and actual practice are a long way apart and that re-emphasis is continually necessary.

Some of these requirements refer to the educational background of school personnel; some are recommendations for studies to implement the program and to demonstrate the necessity of this service to all children. All have been mentioned directly or indirectly throughout this discussion and they are listed now for clarification and emphasis. They have been stressed by teachers, librarians, and administrators in all of the schools visited.

1. Programs for the preparation of elementary teachers should include children's literature courses and should recognize the need for presenting library competencies directly related to the use of library materials in the teaching program. This still remains a number one problem in teacher use of the media center.

2. Elementary school librarians should have a background in elementary education and an understanding of current curriculum trends in order to relate library materials to the needs of teachers and students. A thorough understanding of the role of non-print materials as well as some skill in the use of audio-visual equipment and media must also be a part of their professional education.

3. The education of elementary school administrators should include the elementary school media center program and the responsibility of the administrator to the program. Such courses should relate particularly to budget requirements and the hiring of personnel as well as to the administrator's responsibility to encourage the teachers' use of the library.

4. Studies, both regional and national, should be made of the content of courses offered for the implementation of the first three recommendations. Such studies should be conducted in regular teacher training institutions as well as in liberal arts colleges. These studies should investigate the curriculum, the teaching personnel, and the best methods for insuring the library competencies needed by the teacher before assuming a position in the elementary school.

5. Library services within the elementary school should begin with the youngest class in attendance in order to establish immediately appreciation and understanding of these services which are basic to all future use of libraries and which are an integral part of the child's education. Where necessary, pre-school services should be incorporated.

6. Studies to determine the close affinity between the library program and the reading program within the elementary school; to demonstrate clearly the library's service to the reading program and to present statistics showing this relationship would give impetus to the development of both programs. A good beginning has been made here in the Gaver study[5] but many such studies need to be conducted, involving children in many different types of school communities.

7. An investigation of the relationship between the elementary school library and the programs in the junior and senior high school, both library and otherwise, would be an effective study. It is important to verify statements of librarians that the earlier instruction in library skills increases the learning abilities of the student, as well as his use of the library facilities, as he continues in school.

8. Studies of ways in which other libraries, i.e., children's rooms in public libraries, bookmobiles, etc., may augment the development of elementary school library service should be made. Regional plan-

ning for effective library service is a significant current trend, and the need for cooperation between school libraries and those which serve the child in his out-of-school and later life is an accepted fact. What is needed, however, is a presentation of methods which would develop effectively cooperative services, spelled out in a positive manner. This could do much to advance both phases of library service to children.

9. It has been suggested that the elementary school library must be effectively presented to parents, Boards of Education and other members of the community in a more forceful manner. A study which would show good techniques for developing public relations is urgent. The valuable contribution which the library makes to the basic educational development of the child and the special support which it offers to the enriched program for the gifted child are among the services which could be emphasized. The Knapp report, Realization, is a source which could be used here as a basis for amplification of demonstration centers.[6]

10. Vital to the future growth of the elementary school library is a national emphasis on the importance of providing the space, the budget and the staff necessary to meet the basic guidelines in the new joint Standards for School Media Programs. Federal legislation has given some impetus here but the real growth will come with the implementation at state and local levels of the new Standards.

Conclusion

The answer, therefore, to the question asked by many school administrators and teachers, "Is a program of elementary school library service a possibility for us?" is an affirmative one. The illustrations from on-the-spot observations, the comments and statements by librarians, teachers, administrators, parents and children indicate that such programs are not rarities or ideals but are actualities in a multitude of elementary school situations. They can and should become realities in all.[7] It has been demonstrated that this is a workable program which can be achieved by a coordinated effort on the part of the administrators, the teachers, the parents and the librarian in situations where there is acceptance and an understanding of the educational values inherent in such a facility. There is evidence that elementary school faculties which now have such library service are unanimous in their conviction that this is the one facility necessary to an adequate teaching job for today's children.

"A cooperative approach to directed student learning in a library environment which emphasizes student use of all print and non-print materials plus equipment housed on a local school level," comprises one school's media center program statement, adding,

1. The responsibility for <u>learning</u> is placed upon the student;
2. The responsibility for <u>directed learning</u> is placed upon the teacher and the librarian;
3. The responsibility for the obtainment, organization, and distribution of materials and equipment is placed upon the librarian;
4. The responsibility for the implementation of materials and equipment is shared by the student, the teacher, and the librarian.[8]

With such a foundation as this, the new elementary school library-media center is fast becoming the creative catalyst in education which is its destiny.

Since the library and its resources appear to be of invaluable assistance in this challenging program of educating future citizens, it is hoped that this presentation of methods and techniques for using library services and materials in the elementary school will be of value to those in the academic world who are training future teachers and librarians; to those in the field cur-

Elementary School Libraries Are Realities

rently working with boys and girls in the elementary school community and to parents. Furthermore, it is hoped that these illustrations will encourage teachers and librarians to develop approaches which will lead the individual child to an appreciation and exploration of his inheritance in the world of books and to promote the knowledge which will enable boys and girls to think for themselves. This library foundation becomes of major significance in the development of boys and girls who will be able to meet the problems of future scientific discoveries and idealogical struggles with intelligence and courage and will be able to preserve balance in perpetuating their cultural heritage.

References

1. Bear Creek School, Baltimore County, Maryland.
2. Fairmount School, Jamestown, New York.
3. Stearman School, Wichita, Kansas.
4. Euclid School, Jamestown, New York.
5. Rutgers University. Graduate School of Library Service. Effectiveness of Centralized Library Service in Elementary Schools by Mary Virginia Gaver. 2d ed. New Brunswick, N.J., Rutgers University Press, 1963.
6. Realization: The Final Report of the Knapp School Libraries Project. Editor: Peggy Sullivan. American Library Association, 1968.
7. Mary Virginia Gaver. Patterns of Development in Elementary School Libraries Today: Emerging Media Centers. Third Edition. Encyclopedia Britannica, Inc., 1969.
8. Pinewood School, Wichita, Kansas.

Children's Books Mentioned in Text

Adventures of Tom Sawyer	Samuel Clemens
Alice's Adventures in Wonderland	Lewis Carroll, pseud.
All About Us	Eva Knox Evans
All-Of-A-Kind-Family	Sydney Taylor
Amos Fortune	Elizabeth Yates
Ape In A Cap	Fritz Eichenberg
Beginning Science with Mr. Wizard: Water	Don Herbert and H. Ruchlis
Benjamin Franklin	Clara Ingram Judson
Book of Satellites for You	Franklyn Branley
Boy of the Pyramids	Ruth Jones
Bright April	Marguerite DeAngeli
Bright Design	Katherine Shippen
Caddie Woodlawn	Carol R. Brink
Call it Courage	Armstrong Sperry
Carry on, Mr. Bowditch	Jean Lee Latham
Caves of the Great Hunters	Hans Baumann
Charlotte's Web	Elwyn B. White
Child's History of Art	Virgil Hillyer
Child's History of the World	Virgil Hillyer
Come To The Farm	Ruth M. Tensen
Come To The Zoo	Ruth M. Tensen
Cowboy Small	Lois Lenski
Cowtail Switch, and Other West African Stories	Harold Courlander
Cricket in Times Square	George Selden
Crystal Magic	Eugene David
Curious World of Crystals	Lenore Sanders
Dancing In The Moon	Fritz Eichenberg
Daniel Boone	James Dougherty
Digging Into Yesterday	Estelle Friedman
Door In The Wall	Marguerite DeAngeli
The Duchess Bakes a Cake	Virginia Kahl

Exploring Mars	Roy Gallant
Fabulous Flight	Robert Lawson
Famous Men of Medicine	Caroline Chandler
Famous Paintings	Alice Chase
Farmer Small	Lois Lenski
Find Out About Spring	
Find Out By Touching	Paul Shores
First Book of Bees	Albert B. Tibbets
First Book of Bugs	Margaret Williamson
First Book of Music	Gertrude Norman
First Delights	Tasha Tudor
Four Riders	Charlotte Krum
Four Took Freedom	Philip Sterling and Rayford Logan
A Garden We Planted Together	United Nations
Gift of The Golden Cup	Isabelle Lawrence
Gift of the River	Enid Meadowcroft
A Glorious Age in Africa	Daniel Chu and E. Skinner
Golden Dictionary	Ellen Walpole
Golden Name Day	Jennie Lindquist
Golden Treasury of Natural History	Bertha M. Parker
Good Master	Kate Seredy
Goya	Elizabeth Ripley
Heidi	Johanna Spyri
Hi Mr. Robin	Alvin Tresselt
Homer Price	Robert McCloskey
The Hundred Dresses	Eleanor Estes
The Iliad of Homer	Alfred Church
Incredible Journey	Sheila Burnford
Insect World	Hilda Harpster
Insects	Herbert Zim
International Library of Negro Life and History (5 vols.)	
Island of the Blue Dolphins	Scott O'Dell
Jack Tales	Richard Chase
Jazz Country	Nat Hentoff
Jareb	Miriam Powell
Johnny Tremain	Esther Forbes
Jungle Book	Rudyard Kipling
Junior Book of Insects	Edwin W. Teale
Junket	Anne H. White

Kid Brother	Jerrold Beim
King of The Wind	Marguerite Henry
Kintu	Elizabeth Enright
Kobi	Mary and Conrad Buff
Landing of The Pilgrims	James Dougherty
Lazy Lisa Lizard	Marie Rains
Leonardo Da Vinci	Elizabeth Ripley
Let's Go To The Library	Naomi Buchheimer
Lift Every Voice	Dorothy Sterling and B. Quarles
The Lion, The Witch and The Wardrobe	C. S. Lewis
Little Bear	Else H. Minarik
Little Eddie	Carolyn Haywood
The Little Prince	Antoine de Saint Exupéry
Ludwig Beethoven and The Chiming Bells	Opal Wheeler and Sybil Deucher
Many Moons	James Thurber
Mary Poppins	Pamela Travers
The Matchlock Gun	Walter Edmonds
The Merry Adventures of Robin Hood	Howard Pyle
Microbes At Work	Miriam Selsam
Mike Fink	James Bowman
Mike Mulligan and His Steamshovel	Virginia Lee Burton
Minn of the Mississippi	Holling C. Holling
Miss Flora McFlimsey	Marian C. Foster
Miss Hickory	Carolyn S. Bailey
Miss Pickerell Goes To Mars	Ellen MacGregor
Mister Justice Holmes	Clara Ingram Judson
Misty of Chincoteague	Marguerite Henry
Moby Dick	Herman Melville
Moccasin Trail	William Steele
Modern Medical Discoveries	Irmengarde Eberle
Moon Trip	Michael Chester
(The Story of) Mozart	Helen Kaufmann
My Five Senses	Oliki
Nils	Ingrid and Edgar P. D'Aulaire
The Odyssey of Homer	Alfred Church

Old Yeller	Fred Gipson
One God: The Ways We Worship Him	Florence Mary Fitch
Outline of History	H. G. Wells
Paddle-To-The-Sea	Holling C. Holling
Panuck, Eskimo Sled Dog	Frederick Machetanz
Papa Small	Lois Lenski
People and Their Actions in Social Roles	Presno and Presno
People are Important	Eva Knox Evans
Peter Pan	James M. Barrie
Peterli and The Mountain	Georgia Engelhard
The Phantom Deer	Joseph W. Lippincott
Picture Book of Astronomy	Jerome Meyer
Picture Book of Musical Instruments	Marion Lacey
Plants in The City	Herman L. and Nina Schneider
Prayer For A Child	Rachel Field
Rabbit Hill	Robert Lawson
Rain In The Winds	Claire Louden
Rainbow Dictionary	Wendel William Wright
Rainbow Round The World	Elizabeth Yates
Real Book About Stars	Hal Goodwin
Really Spring	Gene Zion
Red Light, Green Light	Margaret Wise Brown
Robinson Crusoe	Daniel DeFoe
Seeds and Seed Travels	Bertha M. Parker
Sing for America	Opal Wheeler
The Singing Tree	Kate Seredy
Snow Treasure	Marie McSwign
Soldier Doctor	Clara Ingram Judson
Space Cat	Ruthven Todd
Spaceship Under The Apple Tree	Louis Slobodkin
Sparkle and Spin	Ann Rand
Stepsister Sally	Helen F. Daringer
Story of Dr. Dolittle	Hugh Lofting
Story of Mankind	Hendrik Van Loon
Story of Painting for Young People	Horst Janson
Story of the Pennsylvania Dutch	Ann Hark

Strange Visitor	Edith Johnston
Strawberry Girl	Lois Lenski
Superstitious? Here's Why!	Julie Batchelor
This Way To The Stars	John M. Schealer
Three Little Animals	Margaret Wise Brown
Treasure Island	Robert Louis Stevenson
A Tree Is Nice	Janice Udry
True Book of Pets	Ilse Podendorf
The Truth Is One	Henry J. Formann and Roland Gammon
Tune Up	Harriet Huntington
Twenty and Ten	Claire H. Bishop
Voyages of Dr. Dolittle	Hugh Lofting
Voyages of Jacques Cartier	Esther Averill
Watchwords of Liberty	Robert Lawson
Web of Traitors	Geoffrey Trease
What Is Matter	Dan Posin
Wheel On The School	Meindert DeJong
Where Have You Been?	Margaret Wise Brown
Whistle For The Train	Margaret Wise Brown
Whistle For Willie	Ezra Jack Keats
White Stag	Kate Seredy
Wicked John and The Devil	Richard Chase
Wilderness Journey	William O. Steele
Wind In The Willows	Kenneth Grahame
Winnie-The-Pooh	A. A. Milne
Winter Days	William Steele
Wonderful World of Mathematics	Lancelot Hogben
The World's Great Religions	"Life," Editors of
Yellow Magic: The Story of Penicillin	John D. Ratcliff
You and The United Nations	Lois Fisher
You Will Go To The Moon	Mae B. Freeman and Ina B. Freeman

Bibliography

Books and Pamphlets

American Library Association. Committee on Postwar Planning. School Libraries for Today and Tomorrow. Chicago, American Library Association, 1945.

American Association of School Librarians. Dear Mr. Architect: an Open Letter from the School Librarian. Revised ed. Chicago, American Library Association, 1952.

American Association of School Librarians. Standards for School Library Programs. Chicago, American Library Association, 1960.

American Association of School Librarians. Standards for School Media Programs, prepared by the American Association of School Librarians and the Department of Audiovisual Instruction of the National Education Association. Chicago, American Library Association, 1969.

Cecil, Henry L. and Heaps, W. A. School Library Service in the United States. New York, H. W. Wilson Co., 1940.

Cleary, Florence Damon Blueprints for Better Reading. New York, H. W. Wilson Co., 1957.

Crosby, Muriel Estelle, ed. Reading Ladders for Human Relations. Fourth edition. Washington, American Council on Education, 1963.

Darling, Richard L. Public School Library Statistics, 1962-63. U. S. Department of Health, Education and Welfare. U.S. Government Printing Office, 1964.

Developing Permanent Interest in Reading. Helen M. Robinson, ed. Chicago, University of Chicago Press, 1956. (Suppl. Ed. Monograph, No. 84)

Duff, Annis Bequest of Wings; a Family's Pleasures with Books. New York, The Viking Press, 1945.

Duff, Annis Longer Flight; a Family Grows up with Books. New York, The Viking Press, 1955.

Ellsworth, Ralph Eugene The School Library. New York, Center for Applied Research in Education, 1965.

Freund, Roberta Bishop Open the Book. Second edition. Metuchen, N.J.: Scarecrow Press, 1966.

Gaver, Mary Virginia Every Child Needs a School Library. Chicago, American Library Association, 1958.

Gaver, Mary Virginia Patterns of Development in Elementary School Libraries Today: A Five Year Report on Emerging Media Centers. Third edition. Encyclopedia Britannica, Inc., 1969.

Gardiner, Jewel Administering Library Service in the Elementary School. Chicago, American Library Association, 1954.

Growing Up with Books. Compiled in the offices of the Library Journal. New York, R. R. Bowker Co., n. d.

Henne, Frances, Brooks, Alice and Ersted, Ruth. Youth, Communication and Libraries. Chicago, American Library Association, 1949.

Herrick, Virgil E. and Jacobs, Leland B. Children and the Language Arts. Englewood Cliffs, N.J., Prentice Hall, Inc., 1955.

Joint Committee of the National Educational Association and the American Library Association. Schools and Public Libraries Working Together in School Library Service. Washington, National Educational Association, 1941.

Kandel, Isaac Leon The New Era in Education: a Comparative Study. Boston, Houghton Mifflin Co., 1955.

Larrick, Nancy A Parent's Guide to Children's Reading. Garden City, New York, Doubleday, 1955.

Maryland State Department of Education. "School Libraries in Maryland." Maryland School Bulletin. XXXIII, June 1954.

Michaelis, John Udey New Designs for the Elementary School Curriculum. New York, McGraw, 1967.

Mott, Carolyn and Baisden, Leo B. The Children's Book on How to Use Books and Libraries. New York, Charles Scribner's Sons, 1955.

Public Library Association. Standards Committee. Minimum Standards for Public Library Systems, 1966. Prepared by the Standards Committee and sub-committees of the Public Library Association, American Library Association. Chicago, American Library Association, 1967.

Rufsvold, Margaret I. Audio-Visual School Library Service. Chicago, American Library Association, 1949.

Rutgers University. Graduate School of Library Service. Effectiveness of Centralized Library Service in Elementary Schools by Mary Virginia Gaver. Second edition. New Brunswick, New Jersey, Rutgers University Press, 1963.

Sullivan, Peggy, ed. Realization: The Final Report of the Knapp School Libraries Project. Chicago, American Library Association, 1968.

Swarthout, Charlene The School Library as Part of the Instructional System. Metuchen, N.J., Scarecrow Press, 1967.

Van Doren, Mark Liberal Education. New York, Henry Holt and Co., 1943.

Articles and Periodicals

Ahlers, Eleanor E. "Developing Library Skills - Whose Responsibility?" School Activities and the Library, 1958. p. 1-2.

Alexander, William M. "Not Stacks, but a Learning Laboratory." The School Executive, LXXVII:54-5, October, 1957.

Arkley, Rose "Independent Reading for First Grades: A Listing." Elementary English, XLVI:444-65, April, 1969.

Beust, Nora E. "Statistics of Public School Libraries", Chapter 6. Biennial Survey of Education in the United States, 1952-54. U.S. Department of Health, Education and Welfare. Washington, U.S. Government Printing Office, 1957.

Campbell, Roald F. "Articulating Elementary and Secondary Schools." Elementary School Journal, LVIII:257-63, February, 1958.

"Current Trends in School Libraries." Alice Lohrer, issue editor. Library Trends, I, January, 1953.

Eakin, Mary K. "The Elementary-School Library." Elementary School Journal, LIII:427-9, April, 1953.

Falk, Philip H. "Changes in School Library Service to Meet Changes in School Programs." ALA Bulletin, LI:263-7, April, 1957.

Henne, Frances "Training Elementary School Librarians." Junior Libraries, III:12-14, December 15, 1956.

Hodges, Elizabeth O. "Selecting Materials to Support the Curriculum." Childhood Education, XLIII:69-72, October, 1966.

Lettvin, Lorelei Joy "Stories to Dramatize." Elementary English, XXXIX:766-9, December, 1962.

Lowrie, Jean E. "Organization and Operation of School Library Materials Center." Library Trends: Library Uses of the New Media of Communication, C. Walter Stone issue editor, XVI:211-227, October, 1967.

McCuskey, Dorothy "The Curriculum and the Creative Elementary School Library." Wilson Library Bulletin, XXXVII:310-14, December, 1962.

McGuire, Alice Brooks "The Librarian's Role in the Literature Program." Elementary English, XLIV: 468-471, May, 1967.

McGuire, Alice Brooks "School's Magic Carpet." Junior Librarian, III:3-4, December 15, 1956.

National Education Association Department of Elementary School Principals. Elementary School Libraries Today. Thirtieth yearbook. Washington, National Education Association, 1951.

National Education Association Department of Elementary School Principals. Instructional Materials for Elementary Schools. Thirty-fifth yearbook. Washington, National Education Association, 1956.

Peterson, Miriam E. "Helping the Slow Reader." Junior Libraries, III:9-11, December 15, 1956.

Potter, Gladys L. "Our School Libraries and Librarians." ALA Bulletin, XLIX:56-8, February, 1955.

Robinson, Helen M. "Development of Reading Skills." Elementary School Journal, LVIII:269-74, February, 1958.

Rogers, C. D. "Developmental Integration." Elementary English, XLV:1068-70, December, 1968.

Sattley, Helen R. "The Credo of School Libraries." The Saturday Review, XL:74-6, November 16, 1957.

Smith, Benjamin Lee "Nerve Center: The School Library." The School Executive, LXXVII:55-7, October, 1957.

Smith, Benjamin Lee The School Library and the White House Conference. A reprint of an address at the general meeting of the American Association of School Librarians. Philadelphia, July 5, 1955. Published by the Grolier Society for the American Association of School Librarians.

White, Lynn J. "The School Library and the Gifted Child." Library Journal, LXXVIII:1480-3, September 15, 1953.

Willis, Benjamin C. "School Librarian: Coordinator." ALA Bulletin, LI:92-4, February, 1957.

Yoakam, Gerald A. "The Reading Study Approach to Printed Materials." The Reading Teacher, XI:146-51, February, 1958.

"Educational Trends and Media Programs in School Libraries." A reprint of a series of articles from the February 1969 ALA Bulletin.

"Providing School Library Services for the Culturally Disadvantaged." A reprint for the American Association of School Librarians of articles which appeared in the ALA Bulletin. June 1964-January 1965.

Unpublished Material

Austin Schools. Office of Library Consultant. "Library Manual." Austin, Texas, n.d. (Mimeographed.)

Benton, Josephine Moffitt "Reading Aloud in the Home." Library Department, Wichita Public Schools, n.d. (Mimeographed).

Board of Education of Baltimore County. "School Libraries in Baltimore County." Annual report, 1956-1957 session. Towson, Maryland, July, 1957. (Mimeographed).

Bowman School. "Learning Laboratory." Lexington, Massachusetts, n.d. (Offset mimeograph).

Buckner School Library. Wichita Public Schools, Wichita, Kansas, n.d. (Publicity brochure).

"Demonstration School Libraries: A Project of Title II Elementary and Secondary Education Act." State Department of Public Instruction, Raleigh, North Carolina, 1966, 1967.

"The Elementary School Library." Bulletin, Office of the Supervisor of School Libraries, Baltimore County Schools. Towson, Maryland. (Mimeographed)

Evanston School District No. 65, Supervisor of Children's Library Service. "Library Manual." Evanston, Illinois, 1958. (Mimeographed).

Fulton County Elementary School Librarians and Virginia McJenkin. "The Elementary Library Handbook: A Guide for Teaching the Appreciation of Good Books and the Use of the School Library." Second edition. Fulton County School System. Library Department. Atlanta, Georgia, 1960; supplement, 1968.

Georgia State Department of Education. "Every Elementary School Can Have a Library." A report of the Elementary School Library Work Conference, Emory University, August 4-7, 1954. Atlanta, Georgia, 1954. (Mimeographed).

Greensboro Public Schools, Library Department. "Annual Report." Greensboro, North Carolina, 1967. (Mimeographed).

Greensboro Public Schools. "Centralized Ordering, Cataloging and Processing of Library Materials: an Outline." Greensboro, North Carolina, 1967.

"Library Guide." Wichita Public Schools, Curriculum Division, Library Department, n.d. (Mimeographed).

"The Library." Stearman Elementary School, Wichita Public Schools, Wichita, Kansas. (Mimeographed).

Martin, Helen Andrews "Development and Emerging Patterns of Elementary School Libraries in Fulton County, Georgia." Unpublished Master's thesis, School of Library Science, Western Reserve University, 1955.

McGuire, Alice Brooks "Developmental Values in Children's Literature." Unpublished Ph.D. dissertation, Graduate Library School, University of Chicago, 1958.

"Prairie School District Libraries." Prairie Village, Kansas. (Mimeographed).

Superintendent's Bulletin to Classroom Teachers. Evanston School District No. 65. Evanston, Illinois. (Mimeographed).

"Take a Look at Our School Libraries." Board of Education of Baltimore County, Towson, Maryland, 1956. (Processed folder).

Commercial Media Aids

KYE - Know Your Encyclopedia (transparencies prepared by Educational Division, F.E. Compton Co.). Encyclopedia Britannica, Inc., 1964.

The Library - A Place for Discovery (16mm color). Encyclopedia Britannica, Inc., 1966.

Library Series I, II, III, IV (transparencies). Colonial Films, Atlanta, Georgia, 1967.

Using the Library (series of six filmstrips, color). Encyclopedia Britannica, Inc., 1963.

Visuals for Library Instruction. Holyoke, Massachusetts, Technifax Corp., 1960. (26 overhead projectuals by Hoosier Library Transparencies Inc.).

Index

Administrators, school, 153-66
---Achieving good programs, 166
---Education of librarians, 166
---Ideas for expansion, 164-6
---Philosophy of, 154-60
---Responsibilities of, 160-4
---Views on services of librarians, 159-60
---Views on value of library to children, 156-7
    See also Curriculum coordinator; Principals
Aims of elementary school librarians, 11-14, 20-1
Aims of library instruction, 99-100
Appreciation of reading, See Reading guidance
Art, library materials in, 45-6
Art work as reading record, 93
Audio visual aids, See Non-book media
Authors, letters to, 66, 72

Bibliography, 223-30
Biography, 31, 36
Blind children, work with, 55
Book characters, 172
Book clubs, 92
Book collection, 144-5
Book discussions, 64-6
Book fair, 174
Book games, puzzles, quizzes, 68, 92
Book reports, 89-94
Book reviewing, 66
Book Week, 67, 173-4, 197, 200
Book selection, 144-5
Bookmobiles, 17, 203
Bulletins and letters for publicity, 172

Caldecott award books, 64
Card catalog, 106-8

Card files, 87, 90
Centralized elementary school libraries, 12-16, 21
Children's books mentioned in text, 218-22
Classics, interest in, 67-8
Clerical needs, 183
Community relationships, 191-207
---Community agencies, 206-7
---Parent relationships, 191-203
---Public library cooperation, 203-6
Creative expression, 83-6
Culturally deprived, 55-6
Curriculum coordinator, 158
Curriculum support (middle grades), 20-50
---Art, 45-6
---Audio visual aids, 28
---Biography, use of, 31, 36
---Blind, work with, 55
---Culturally disadvantaged, 55-6
---Encyclopedia, use of, 29-31
---Fiction, use in social studies, 29-30, 38, 50
---Gifted children, 24, 47-51
---Health, 44-45
---Interracial materials, 30
---Learning resources center, 55-6
---Library practices, 15, 20-5
---Library resources, 28-31
---Mathematics, 46
---Mentally retarded, 52-4
---Music, 46
---Nature study, 40-42
---Note taking, 26-8
---Physically handicapped, 54-5
---Pre-planning in classroom, 25
---Safety, 45-6
---Science, 40-4
---Slow learners, 51-4
---Social studies, 31-40
---Using library materials, 25-8

Dewey decimal, 101, 106, 109-11
Dictionary, 106
Disadvantaged, See Culturally deprived
Displays, 64, 66, 70, 170

Early Elementary library services, 122-42
---Audio visual tapes, 141
---Curriculum support, 137-8
---First grade experiences, 125-35
---Independent reading, 134
---Introduction to library tools, 100-1, 133, 135, 139
---ITA, 134
---Kindergarten experiences, 123-5
---Literary appreciation, 140-2
---Nongraded programs, 139
---Objectives, 122
---Parent cooperation, 123, 125-30, 132-3
---Pre-school, 122, 124
---Reading guidance, 136, 138
---Reading records, 130, 137
---Science interests, 136
---Second grade experiences, 135-7
---Story hours, 140-2
---Third grade experiences, 137-9
Elementary school libraries, 11-18, 210-17
---Administrators attitudes, 153-66
---Aims of, 11-14, 20-1, 122
---Centralized, 12-16, 21
---Children's attitudes, 211
---Future study needs, 212-5
---Growth and scope, 12-18, 216-17
---Parents' attitudes, 201-3
---Services summarized, 212
---Teachers' attitudes, 210-11
Encyclopedia, use of, 29-31, 108-9

Fiction, use of, 29-30 38, 50
Field trips, 53, 72
Fifth grade, reading guidance, 75-7
Fifth grade, social studies, 34-6
First grade experiences, 125-35
---Introduction to library tools, 133, 135
---Reading records, 130
Fourth grade, reading guidance, 69-75
Fourth grade, social studies, 32-4

Gifted children, 24, 47-51
Group guidance in reading, 64-8

233

Growth and scope of elementary libraries, 12-18, 216-17

Headstart programs, See Pre-school programs
Health materials, 44-5
Hobbies as incentive to reading, 60
Home reading, 76, 196-201

Independent reading, 134
Individual reading guidance, 62-4
ITA, 134
Inservice training for teachers, 149-50
Interracial materials, 30

Kindergarten-primary library objectives, 122
Kindergarten experiences, 123-5

Learning resource center, 55-6
   See also Media services; Physical facilities
Librarians' responsibility for teacher-librarian cooperation, 148-9
Library citizenship, 100, 111-12
Library club, 67
   See also Student assistants
Library instruction, 99-114
---Alphabetizing, 101
---Appreciation of reading, See Reading guidance
---Card catalog, 106-8
---Desired outcomes, 99-100
---Dewey decimal, 101, 109-11
---Dictionary, 106
---Encyclopedia, 108-9
---Librarian's presentation, 35, 39, 43
---Library citizenship, 100, 111-12
---Placement chart of activities, 102-5
---Primary grades, 100-1
---Skill reviews, 113-14
---Teacher presentations, 105
---Use of audio visual aids, 100, 112-13
---Use of reference books, 118-20
Library program, 15, 20-5
Library resources, 28-31
Library skills, primary grades, 100-1, 135, 139
Library skills reviewed, 113-14

Literary appreciation, early elementary, 140-2
  See also Reading guidance

Making a book, 72-3
Mathematics, library materials, 46
Media services, 184-7
---Dial access, 186
---ETV, 185, 186
---Listening stations, 186
---Organization, 184
---Tapes, 185
---Transparencies, 185
  See also Non-book media, use of
Mentally retarded, 52-4
Music library materials, 46

Nature study, 40-2
Newbery award books, 64
Non-book media, use of, 28, 33, 45, 53, 55, 78, 80, 84, 91, 100, 112-13, 122, 125, 141, 154, 155, 171, 172, 193, 199. See also Media services
Non graded programs, 139, 145
Note taking, 26-8

Paperbacks, 51, 68
Parent cooperation, primary level, 123, 125-30, 132-33
Parent relationships to library, 76, 173, 191-203
---Assistance from, 191-4
---Assistance to, 195-201
---Attitudes toward, 201-3
Parent shelf, 196, 199
Philosophy of school administrators, 154-60
Physical facilities, 187-9
Physically handicapped, 54-5
Placement chart of library activities, 102-5
Poetry appreciation, 80-3
Pre-planning, teacher-librarian, 24-5, 32, 73, 145-6
Pre-school programs, 122-4, 206
Principals, 162-4. See also Administrators, school
Professional shelf, 149
PTA, See Parent relationships
Public library, cooperation with, 203-6
Publicity, 169-74

---Book characters, 172
---Book week, 173-4, 197, 200
---Book fair, 174
---Bulletins and letters, 172
---Displays, 170
---Newspaper, 171
---Radio, 172
Puppet plays, 94

Reading aloud, 71-2, 76
Reading, time provided for, 15, 70, 72, 75, 79
Reading guidance, 60-94
---Art work, 93
---Book clubs, 92
---Book discussions, 64-6
---Book games, puzzles, etc., 68
---Book reports, 89-94
---Book Week assembly, 67
---Booklets, 88
---Card files, 87, 90
---Choosing books to help solve child's similar problems, 63, 66
---Classroom programs, 68-80
---Creative expression, 83-6, 78
---Desired outcomes, 60-2, 94-5
---Displays, 64, 66, 70
---Early elementary, 123-5, 136, 138, 140-2
---Fourth grade, 69-75
---Fifth grade, 75-9
---Group guidance by librarian, 64-8
---Help of teachers, 68-80
---Home reading, 76
---Individual guidance by librarian, 62-4
---Letters to authors, 66, 72
---Making a book, 72-3
---Poetry appreciation, 80-3
---Puppet plays, 94
---Reading aloud, 71-2, 76
---Reading records, 86-94
---Recordings, 78, 80
---Review new books, 66
---Riddles, 92
---Sharing aloud, 71, 77
---Sixth grade, 79-80

---Story hours, 64, 77-8
---Tape recorder, 91
---Types of material, 84-5
Reading interests, 74-5, 78, 80
Reading records, 86-94, 130, 137
Recordings, 78, 80
Reference books, use of, 118-120
Reference work, 24, 27, 114-20
References to schools visited, 56-9, 95-8, 120-1, 142-3, 151-2, 166-8, 189-90, 207-9, 217

Safety, materials in, 45
Scheduling, 174-9
---Flexible programs, 176-8
School libraries, See Elementary school libraries
Science, 40-4, 136
---Nature study, 40-2
Scope of elementary school libraries, 12-8, 216-7
Second grade experiences, 135-7
---Reading interests, 136
---Reading records, 137
---Science interests, 136
Sharing books aloud, 71, 77
Sixth grade experiences, 79-80
Sixth grade social sciences, 36-40
Slow learners, 51-4
Social studies, 31-40
---Ancient civilizations and world people, 36-40
---Fiction, used in, 29-30, 38, 50
---Fifth grade, 34-6
---Fourth grade, 32-4
---People in other lands, 32-4
---Sixth grade, 36-40
---United States, 34-6
Story hours, 64, 77, 78, 140-2, 206
Student assistants, 179-84
---Library council, 183
Student teachers, 147

Teacher-librarian cooperation, 144-51
---Book selection, 144-5
---Inservice orientation, 149-50
---Library responsibilities, 148-9

---Non graded programs, 145
---Pre-planning, 145-6
---Professional shelf, 149
---Student teaching programs, 147
---Teacher background in children's literature, 150-5
---Teacher participation in library, 146-8
Teachers attitudes, 210-11
Teachers background in children's literature, 150-1
Teachers role in reading guidance, 68-80, 105
Team teaching, 145
Third grade experiences, 137-9
---Advanced reading interests, 138
---Curriculum support, 137-8

Vacation reading plans, 204

Z
675
S3L88
1970

APR 17 1970